Organized Crime and Illicit Trade

Virginia Comolli
Editor

Organized Crime and Illicit Trade

How to Respond to This Strategic Challenge
in Old and New Domains

Editor
Virginia Comolli
International Institute for Strategic Studies
London, UK

ISBN 978-3-030-10293-7   ISBN 978-3-319-72968-8   (eBook)
https://doi.org/10.1007/978-3-319-72968-8

Cover pattern © Melisa Hasan

Printed on acid-free paper

This Palgrave Macmillan imprint is published by Springer Nature
The registered company is Springer International Publishing AG
The registered company address is: Gewerbestrasse 11, 6330 Cham, Switzerland

ACKNOWLEDGMENTS

This book grew out of a project run jointly by the Security and Development Programme and the Geo-economics and Strategy Programme at The International Institute for Strategic Studies (IISS) and made possible thanks to the support of HSBC and British American Tobacco.

The initial activity of the project was an off-the-record international conference on the strategic implications of organized criminal markets hosted at IISS-Middle East in Manama, Kingdom of Bahrain in 2015. The aim of the initiative was to strengthen international understanding of transnational organized crime and its implications; discuss solutions based on on-the-ground experience and concrete case studies; and facilitate the sharing of ideas and best practice among different stakeholders.

I am indebted to the 45 senior government and law-enforcement officials, business leaders, representatives from international organisations and influential experts from countries as varied as Colombia, India, Japan, Mali, Georgia, Taiwan and the United States, among others, who attended the event, shared their knowledge and provided the initial input for the content of this volume.

Particularly, I am grateful to Dr Vanda Felbab-Brown, Dr Camino Kavanagh, Karl Lallerstedt, and Tuesday Reitano who had presented drafts of their papers in Bahrain, actively engaged in stimulating discussions and produced the chapters that appear in the following pages. These have benefited from extensive feedback from conference participants as well as the authors' many years of experience, field research and engagement with policymakers, the corporate sector, security, defence and development practitioners, and the expert community.

London   Virginia Comolli
May 2017

CONTENTS

LIST OF CONTRIBUTORS

Virginia Comolli is the Senior Fellow for Security and Development The International Institute for Strategic Studies. She is the author of *Boko Haram: Nigeria's Islamist Insurgency* (Hurst, 2015) and co-author with Nigel Inkster of *Drugs, Insecurity and Failed States: the Problems of Prohibition* (Routledge, 2012).

Vanda Felbab-Brown is a Senior Fellow in the Center for 21st Century Security and Intelligence in the Foreign Policy program at the Brookings Institution. She is the author of, among others, *Narco Noir: Mexico's Cartels, Cops, and Corruption* (Brookings Institution Press, 2016); *Aspiration and Ambivalence: Strategies and Realities of Counterinsurgency and State-Building in Afghanistan* (Brookings Institution Press, 2012) and *Shooting Up: Counterinsurgency and the War on Drugs* (Brookings Institution Press, 2010).

Camino Kavanagh is an international consultant and currently serves as Advisor a number of organisations including the UN Group of Governmental Experts on Cyber Security, the ICT4 Peace Foundation, the West Africa Commission on Drugs (WACD) and the National Committee on US Foreign Policy (NCAFP). She is a non-resident Fellow at the Center on International Cooperation and a Board Member of the Global Initiative on Transnational Crime.

Karl Lallerstedt is the Programme Director for Illicit Trade, Financial and Economic Crime at the Global Initiative against Transnational Organized Crime. He is also the co-founder of Black Market Watch and a member of the OECD Task Force on Charting Illicit Trade. Among others, he has prior experience in anti-illicit trade in the corporate sector.

Tuesday Reitano is the Deputy Director of the Global Initiative against Transnational Organized Crime and a Senior Research Associate at the Institute for Security Studies in Pretoria. Formerly Head of the Secretariat of the Global Initiative against Transnational Organized Crime and working for a number of UN agencies, Tuesday is the lead author for the OECD-DAC 2016 Flagship publication on illicit financial flows emanating from illicit trade in West Africa.

LIST OF ACRONYMS

ACTA   Anti-Counterfeiting Trade Agreement
AQIM   al-Qaeda in the Islamic Maghreb
ARPANET   Advanced Research Projects Agency Network
ASD2030   2030 Agenda for Sustainable Development
BMR   BlackMarket Reloaded
CALEA   Communications Assistance for Law Enforcement Act
CICIG   International Commission against Impunity in Guatemala
            (Spanish: *Comisión Internacional contra la Impunidad en Guatemala*)
DARPA   Defense Advanced Research Projects Agency
DEA   Drug Enforcement Administration
ECOWAS   Economic Community of West African States
EU   European Union
EUROPOL   European Police Office
FARC   Revolutionary Armed Forces of Colombia (Spanish: *Fuerzas Armadas Revolucionarias de Colombia*)
FBI   Federal Bureau of Investigation
FCC   Federal Communications Commission
FSB   Federal Security Service
GDP   gross domestic product
GFI   Global Financial Integrity
ICC   International Chamber of Commerce
ICT   Information Communications Technology

IDEA	International Institute for Democracy and Electoral Assistance
IEEPA	International Emergency Economic Powers Act
IFF	Illicit financial flows
IMF	International Monetary Fund
IP	Intellectual property
ISIS	Islamic State of Iraq and al-Sham
ISP	Internet service provider
IT	information technology
IUU	Illegal, unreported and unregulated
MDG	Millennium Development Goal
MLAT	Mutual legal assistance treaty
NATO	North Atlantic Treaty Organization
NGO	non-governmental organisation
NYPD	New York Police Department
OAS	Organisation of American States
ODA	Official development assistance
OECD	Organisation for Economic Co-operation and Development
ONDCP	Office of National Drug Control Policy
PCC	First Capital Command (Portuguese: *Primeiro Comando da Capital*)
PIRA	Provisional Irish Republican Army
PKK	Kurdistan Workers' Party (Kurdish: *Partiya Karkerên Kurdistanê*)
PRI	Institutional Revolutionary Party (Spanish: *Partido Revolucionario Institucional*)
R&D	Research and development
RICO	Racketeer Influenced and Corrupt Organisations
SDG	Sustainable Development Goal
SDN	Specially Designated Narcotics Trafficker
SIU	Special interdiction unit
TOSD	total official support for development
UK	United Kingdom
UN	United Nations
UNODC	United Nations Office on Drugs and Crime
UNTOC	United Nations Convention against Transnational Organized Crime
US	United States

USAID	United States Agency for International Development
VPN	Virtual private networks
WCO	World Customs Organisation
WEF	World Economic Forum
WHO	World Health Organisation
WIPO	World Intellectual Property Organization

INTRODUCTION: A STRATEGIC CHALLENGE

Abstract In the opening chapter the editor introduces the volume and explains what differentiates the book from other work on the subject. Specifically, she explains how the ensuing pages are less concerned with *the problem* of organized crime as they are with understanding the implications of the phenomenon. Most people would agree that criminal activities are *bad* but the following chapters will answer the questions of 'how?', 'for whom?' and, controversially, 'are they always bad?'.

Keywords Organized crime • Development • Responses

As I watch popular TV show *Narcos* I cannot help but feel some disbelief as I am reminded of Pablo Escobar's shenanigans, how the infamous Medellin Cartel came to be and, above all, the grip that this man—the then richest in the world according to *Forbes*—and his associates held over Colombian civilians, police, military, media and political elite in the 1970s and 1980s. Setting aside TV dramatisation, Escobar's multi-million dollar business, brutal violence and political ambitions are well documented and the fear that the country would become a fully-fledged narco-state was very real.

Fast forward to the 2010s, Escobar's Cartel has long been dismantled and Medellin is cited around the world as a positive albeit imperfect example of urban transformation. But yet drug trafficking organisations are hardly a feature of the past. This is not only true for places such as Mexico where 23,000 homicides where registered in 2016—a large proportion of which was deemed to be organized crime-related.[1] The peaceful Netherlands were the set of one of the most innovative developments in the business in recent years. In 2013 it emerged that computer hackers had been hired by drug traffickers to breach the information technology (IT) system of Antwerp port control system to ensure that tons of narcotics would go undetected among regular cargos. The novelty of this case was represented by the fact that unlike regular cyber-crime—to which we are becoming increasingly accustomed—in this instance cyber capabilities had been used to facilitate real-life physical criminal activities.

Indeed, over time criminals have been known for using all available tools to carry out their activities making the most of technological advances as well as pre-existing circumstances and new opportunities. These could be anything from a weak judiciary, a favourable topography, or the unprecedented spike in the number of refugees prepared to do almost anything to escape the horrors of conflict and find safety in Europe. Here lies the challenge of designing effective counter-strategies that are equally broad-ranging and imaginative.

Much has been written about organized crime, a problem whose exact definition is still somehow elusive and up for debate to the point that it can vary quite significantly from country to country—as Interpol itself acknowledges. For one, I find useful the definition adopted by the British Home Office which regards organized crime as criminal activities involving two of more individuals over a period of time (rather than on a one-off basis), often across national borders, usually (but not always) for financial gain.[2] Increasingly, technological tools are used in the planning and execution of such activities which are characterised by a certain degree of diversification, as exemplified by so-called poly-crime groups. One could also add that, in contrast to the actions of small-time criminals, the often high-level penetration of which organized crime is capable within societies—intended as political, business and social circles—is a key differential and one that will be explored in detail in the coming chapters.

Nevertheless, and unlike much of the existing literature on the subject, this book is not as much about *the problem* of organized crime as it is focused on understanding the implications of the phenomenon. Most people would agree that criminal activities are *bad* but the following chapters will answer the questions of 'how?', 'for whom?' and, controversially, 'are they always bad?'. The true and multi-faceted impact of transnational organized crime calls for higher policy prioritisation and mainstreaming of what Karl Lallerstedt later labels a 'mega-problem' (Chap. 4). The ensuing pages will stress that despite a plethora of competing national and international priorities and crises that impact security, the economic system and diplomatic relations, transnational organized crime has repercussions that are so deep and wide that virtually no sector—and certainly no region in the world—can consider itself untouched. Indeed, many of the international challenges facing the world today—being them the conflict in Syria and the rise of the Islamic State of Iraq and al-Sham (ISIS) or the Ukrainian crisis—have substantial criminal components. It follows that gone are the days when governments could afford to regard organized crime exclusively as the realm of law enforcement and, as such, as less of a strategic threat.

Starting with the military, which is increasingly involved in law enforcement roles, development agencies, technology companies, financial institutions, the health sector, and many other 'non-traditional crime-fighters' have a role to play in devising responses to what is a truly strategic challenge of our time. One that erodes governance systems, builds parallel economies rivalling licit markets, undermines public health, destroys the environment, and fuels violence acting as an accelerant of conflict and sponsor of violent extremism. Furthermore, as criminals intersect with other malign actors such as insurgents, terrorists, and some authoritarian states, they become part of that range of hybrid challenges that, as Vanda Felbab-Brown will later elucidate (Chap. 1), more and more frequently governments are compelled to address in the twenty-first century. In a similar vein, as early as in 2004 the UN High Level Panel on Threats and Challenges identified organized crime as one of six clusters of threats the world had to prioritize for decades to come, alongside civil wars, terrorism, and nuclear proliferation.[3]

Playing Catch-Up

The constant struggle of matching opponent's capabilities is a real one and varies considerably from state to state. Albeit not in itself an existential threat, the Antwerp incident described earlier is indicative of the appeal enjoyed by cyber tools as they can provide *strategic advantages* to those non-state actors employing them. But perhaps more significantly, it appears that their existence and use have prompted a power shift in the relationship between criminals and law enforcement agencies. Whereas organized criminal groups worldwide had repeatedly shown the ability to use the internet and other technologies, dozens of countries lack specialised centres to counter cyber crime; not to mention the speed with which criminals appear to find loopholes in law-enforcement systems and regulations, adapting their operations accordingly. For these reasons, Camino Kavanagh devotes an extended discussion (Chap. 3) to tracing the origins of cyber crime and, more importantly, how IT and cyber tools have been used as enablers of global illicit trade—a trend that had become increasingly visible starting in the early 2000s.

If Western nations struggle to keep-up with highly adaptable criminal networks, emerging and developing countries risk being overwhelmed by criminal infiltration and collusion as exemplified by the often-cited case of Guinea-Bissau.[4] Here, the president and the army chief of staff were killed in 2009 in what was believed to be a settling of scores related to the control of the narcotics trade. If this was not enough, the navy chief of staff was designated by Washington as an international drug kingpin and eventually arrested in 2013. He has since pleaded guilty (secretly).[5] Although the Bissau-Guinean case might have been the one in the limelight, a closer examination suggests that, albeit to a lesser extent, elsewhere in the continent the problems of criminal infiltration are very tangible, including in countries that are commonly perceived as success stories. In Ghana, for instance, drug proceeds have been used to support the election of members of parliament, weakening their accountability and obviously undermining democratic institutions.[6] As Tuesday Reitano will explain, this is only one of the ways in which the presence of organized criminal networks undermines development (Chap. 2). Indeed, the role crime plays hindering socio-economic progress and fuelling instability in regions experiencing or recovering from conflict has been recognised in the post-2015 Sustainable Development Agenda agreed in September 2015. Cognisant of the missed opportunity resulting from not including the issue of organized crime in the discussions around the Millennium Development Goals set in 2000, the new agenda stresses that organized crime in its many forms is a clear challenge to development. As a result, it is more important than ever that a combination of security and development initiatives are developed in conjunction, and as part of, a comprehensive approach that encompasses local interventions but also the involvement of foreign donors and partners. Moreover, in light of the greater appreciation of the impact of transnational organized crime on communities, bottom-up approaches should complement more traditional strategies implemented through and by the state.

What to Do

Recommendations on how to develop such approaches will be presented by both Reitano and Felbab-Brown (Chaps. 5 and 6). These will include looking at organized crime in a different light and designing responses that take into account the state-building function performed by criminal non-state actors in places where weak states are unable to provide for their citizenry, hence creating governance and economic vacuums eagerly filled by criminals. The latter, as a result, come to enjoy a degree of legitimacy in the eye of the population that often surpasses the one of formal institutions. Ignoring these dynamics would be missing the strategic extent of criminal implications.

International Institute for Strategic Studies   Virginia Comolli
London, UK

Notes

1. IISS, *The IISS Armed Conflict Survey* (London: Routledge, 2017), p. 344.
2. Hannah Mills, Sara Skodbo and Peter Blyth, 'Understanding organised crime: estimating the scale and the social and economic costs', *Home Office Research Report 73*, October 2013, pp. 5–6.
3. United Nations, *Report of the High-level Panel on Threats, Challenges and Change. A More Secure World: Our Shared Responsibility* (New York: United Nations, 2004).
4. 'Guinea-Bissau president shot dead', *BBC News*, 2 March 2009, http://news.bbc.co.uk/1/hi/world/africa/7918061.stm.
5. Nate Raymond, 'Exclusive: Guinea-Bissau's ex-navy chief pleads guilty in U.S. drug case', Reuters, 3 June 2014, http://www.reuters.com/article/us-bissau-drugs-guilty-idUSKBN0EE2FO20140603; *United States of America v. Jose Americo Bubo Na Tchuto, Papis Djeme, and Tchamy Yala*, Sealed Superseding Indictment, S1 12 Cr. 972, 2014, http://www.justice.gov/sites/default/files/usao-sdny/legacy/2015/03/25/U.S.%20v.%20Na%20Tchuto%20et%20al%20Indictment.pdf.
6. 'Drug money 'tainting Ghana poll'', *BBC News*, 28 October 2008, http://news.bbc.co.uk/1/hi/world/africa/7695981.stm.

CHAPTER 1

The Threat of Illicit Economies and the Complex Relations with State and Society

Vanda Felbab-Brown

Abstract The chapter introduces the multifaceted threat posed by illicit economies and repercussions in the political, economic, environmental and security spheres. It also discusses the relationship between the state and criminal entities, highlighting the ways in which this relationship can be far from antagonistic in nature. A number of case studies show the way in which criminal organisations and governing elites often develop a mutually beneficial accommodation.

The chapter explores the relationship between society and crime, suggesting that large populations around the world in areas with inadequate or problematic state presence, great poverty, and social and political marginalisation are dependent on illicit economies for economic survival and the satisfaction of other socio-economic needs. In this context criminal and belligerent actors become providers of public goods.

Keywords Crime • Drug • Hybrid • State • Society

V. Felbab-Brown (✉)
The Brookings Institution, Washington, DC, USA

© The Author(s) 2018
V. Comolli (ed.), *Organized Crime and Illicit Trade*,
https://doi.org/10.1007/978-3-319-72968-8_1

1

Large-scale illicit economies and intense organized crime have received intense attention from governments and international organisations since the end of the Cold War. The end of Cold War brought a permissive strategic environment that allowed many states to focus on a broader menu of interests in their foreign policy agendas, such as the fight against drug trafficking and production. The reduction of Cold War aid to countries in the midst of the competition between the United States and the Soviet Union exposed the great fragility and institutional underdevelopment of many of these states, a deficiency perhaps exacerbated by globalisation. At the same time, criminal and belligerent actors of significant power but previously hidden in the shadows of Cold War politics were spotlighted by the international community—especially when their activities were associated with the emergence of new situations of intensely violent organized crime or trafficking-related corruption.

The focus on organized crime, illicit economies, and the multiple threats they pose to states and societies further intensified after 9–11 when it became obvious that belligerent groups, such as the Taliban in Afghanistan and Pakistan and the so-called Islamic State of Iraq and al-Sham (ISIS) in Iraq and Syria, derive multiple benefits, including extensive financial profits, from participating in illicit economies, such as the drug trade. In addition to expanding the resources of terrorist and belligerent groups, the persistence and growth of illegal economies also have come to complicate post-conflict stabilisation and reconstruction efforts in countries that have emerged from civil wars—be they Cambodia or Haiti.[1]

Increasingly, the United Nations Security Council has highlighted organized crime as an issue requiring the coordinated focus of various UN bodies and of the Secretary General.[2] The escalation of violence in Central America where weak states have been overwhelmed by the intensity of organized crime, the emergence of drug smuggling in West Africa, which contributes to its cauldron of other illegal economies and poor governance, and the deep penetration of illegal economies into the political and economic life of Afghanistan and Pakistan; massive poaching of animals in Africa and East Asia; ISIS illegally trading in antiquities and oil; and cybercrime around the world have captured policy attention. After leather-clad biker gang Night Wolves helped Russian special operations forces annex Crimea in 2014 and other criminal gang 'volunteers' directed by Russian intelligence agents played a crucial role in Eastern Ukraine, the North Atlantic Treaty Organisation (NATO) too has come to focus strongly on so-called hybrid threats.[3] There is no one accepted definition of hybrid threats, but they all feature the "merger of different modes and means of war,"[4] such as an overlap of non-state militant actors working for or with state military forces or mixtures of insurgency and criminality. The use of organized crime actors by states during conflict or for political control is, of course, nothing new: United States forces invading Sicily in the Second World War relied on the mafia for combat intelligence provision as well as post-invasion stability; Chiang-Kai Shek depended on Du Yuesheng's Green Gang for fighting the Japanese and even made Du, the world's most accomplished drug trafficker, his minister of counternarcotics.[5]

Yet despite the fact that the intersections of crime, conflict, and political rule are not new and that states often have intimate knowledge of using organized crime for their purposes and exploiting illicit economies, many policy interventions to combat organized crime and illicit economies—whether linked to violent conflict or its absence—often have not been highly effective. Paradoxically, at times the policies have turned out to be counterproductive with respect to other objectives, such as mitigating violent conflict, fostering good governance, and promoting human rights, and at times even counterproductive with respect to the objective of weakening criminal groups and their linkages to terrorist organisations.

This is because although illicit economies pose multiple threats to states, even as they are used by them, their effects on societies are often highly complex. Indeed, large populations around the world in areas with inadequate or problematic state presence, great poverty, and social and political marginalisation continue to be dependent on illicit economies, including the drug trade, for economic survival and the satisfaction of other socioeconomic needs. For many, participation in informal economies, if not outright illegal ones, is the only way to satisfy their human security and to provide any chance of their social advancement, even as they continue to exist in a trap of insecurity, criminality, and marginalisation.

A Multifaceted Challenge

Large-scale illicit economies generate multiple threats to states. They can threaten the state *politically* by providing an avenue for criminal organisations and corrupt politicians to enter the political space, undermining the democratic process. These actors, who enjoy the financial resources and political capital generated by sponsoring the illicit economy, frequently experience great success in the political process. They are able to secure official positions of power as well as wield influence from behind the scenes. Consequently, the legitimacy of the political process is subverted. The problem perpetuates itself as successful politicians bankrolled with illicit money make it more difficult for other actors to resist participating in the illicit economy, leading to endemic corruption at both the local and national levels.

Large illicit economies with powerful traffickers also have a pernicious effect on the *judicial* system of the country. First, as the extent of the illicit economy rises, the investigative capacity of the law enforcement and judicial systems diminishes. Impunity for criminal activity also increases, undermining the credibility of the judicial system, its crime-deterring role, and the authority of the government generally. Second, powerful traffickers frequently turn to violent means to deter and avoid prosecution, killing off or bribing prosecutors, judges, and witnesses.[6] Of course, efforts to suppress the production of illicit drugs sometimes also lead to an increase in government human rights abuses.[7]

While the detrimental effects of intense crime and large-scale illicit economies on the political processes are apparent, it is a significant and often inappropriate leap of analysis to assume that the emergence of organized crime and extensive illicit economies will always necessarily challenge political stability and threaten the existing governments and power of ruling elites. To the extent that external drug traffickers make alliances with former or existing rebels not linked to the official system or young challengers who seek social mobility in an exclusive system, the traffickers will develop a conflictual relationship with the state, and political instability may well follow. To the extent that the governing elite captures the new drug rents, a symbiosis between external (and internal) drug traffickers and the ruling elites may develop. Drug traffickers will enjoy a sponsored safe-haven; and while democratic processes and institutional development of the county will be threatened, (ironically!) political stability and the existing political dispensation may well be strengthened.

Illicit economies also have large *economic* effects—not all of them negative. Drug cultivation and processing, for example, on the one hand generate employment for the poor rural population, numbering frequently in the hundreds of thousands. Moreover, not only does the drug economy allow the impoverished poor to make ends meet, it also facilitates upward mobility for many participants.

But a burgeoning drug economy also contributes to inflation and hence can harm legitimate, export-oriented, import-substituting industries.

In Gambia, for example, the influx of external dollars from the illicit drug trade set off significant inflation. It encourages real estate speculation and a rapid rise in real estate prices, and undermines currency stability. It also displaces legitimate production. Since the drug economy is economically superior to legitimate production not only in price profitability, but also requiring less developed infrastructure and not imposing large sunk and transaction costs, the local population is frequently uninterested in, or unable to, participate in other forms of economic activity. The existence of a large illicit economy thus complicates efforts at local development and crowds out legitimate economic activity. The illicit economy can thus lead to the so-called Dutch disease where a boom in an isolated sector of the economy causes or is accompanied by stagnation in other core sectors since it gives rise to appreciation of land and labour costs. Finally, it appears that the small share of the final profits that is captured by the country producing the illicit commodity is used mainly for unproductive consumption by the traffickers, rather than productive economic investment.[8]

Certain illicit economies also create *environmental* threats. Poaching and smuggling of wildlife throughout Africa as well as South East Asia, for example, depletes biodiversity and contributes to the demise of endangered species. Illegal logging in East and West Africa leads to further soil erosion and desertification, making land inhospitable for agriculture. In the Congo and Amazon, illegal logging and mining decimates some of the world's last rain forests, contributes to carbon release and global warming, and species loss. Coca cultivation in Latin America too results in deforestation, and the processing of coca leaves into cocaine leaks highly toxic materials, such as kerosene, into the waterways of some of the richest ecosystems in the world. Illicit smuggling of toxic waste into Africa generates critical health problems and ecological catastrophes, such as happened in the Cote d'Ivoire port of Abidjan in August 2006.[9]

Finally, the presence of a large-scale illicit economy in the context of violent conflict greatly exacerbates *security* threats to the state.[10] And under some circumstances, organized crime can become so violent and so overwhelm a state's weak law enforcement capacity that its actions can amount to a national security, not merely a public safety, threat to the state. Belligerent groups that embrace illicit economies, such as the Taliban in Afghanistan, the Sendero Luminoso in Peru, the Fuerzas Armadas Revolucionarias de Colombia (FARC) and the paramilitaries in Colombia, derive a multitude of benefits from such illicit economies. With the large

profits they derive, belligerents improve the physical resources they have
to fight the state: they can hire more combatants, pay them better salaries,
and equip them with better weapons. In fact, the increase in the belligerents' physical resources is frequently immense; in the case of the FARC
and the officially-demobilised paramilitaries in Colombia, for example, the
financial profits from drugs are on average estimated at about USD100
million a year, or between 50% and 70% of the groups' incomes.[11]

Better procurement and logistics also enhance what can be called 'the
freedom of action' of belligerents, that is, the scope of tactical options
available to them and their ability to optimize both tactics and their grand
strategy. Prior to penetrating illicit economies, belligerents frequently have
to deplete much time and energy on activities that do little to advance
their cause, such as robbing banks and armouries to obtain money and
weapons, or extorting the local population for food supplies. Once their
participation in an illicit economy, such as the drug trade, solves the belligerents' logistics and procurement needs, they become free to concentrate on high-value, high-impact targets.

Critically, participation in illicit economies greatly increases the belligerents' political capital, that is the extent to which the population wel-
comes and tolerates the presence of the belligerents. Large-scale illicit
economies frequently provide basic livelihood for the population in a conflict zone, and by sponsoring the illicit economy, belligerents are able to
distribute real-time economic benefits to the population. Moreover, as
indicated above, beyond the basic provision of livelihoods, belligerents
also provide protection and regulation services to the illicit economy and
its producers against, for instance, brutal and unreliable traffickers. With
large financial profits from the illicit economy, belligerents also often provide a variety of otherwise-absent social services, as did Peru's Shining
Path during the 1980s, such as clinics, roads, and schools.[12]

Four factors have a decisive influence on the extent to which belligerent
groups derive political capital from their sponsorship of illicit economies:
the state of the overall economy in the country/region; the character of
the illicit economy; the presence or absence of independent traffickers;
and the government's response to the illicit economy.

The *state of the overall economy* determines the extent to which the local
population is dependent on the illicit economy for basic livelihood and any
chance of social advancement. The poorer the country and the smaller the
size and accessibility of the licit economy, on the one hand, the greater is
the dependence of the population on the illicit one, and the greater is the

political capital that accrues to belligerents for sponsoring the illicit economy. On the other hand, in a rich developed country with a plenitude of legal economic opportunities, the larger population may well object to the illicit economy and the belligerents' participation in it can discredit them. Hence, in Afghanistan today, the Taliban derives substantial political capital from its protection of the poppy fields. This political capital is all the more vital for the Taliban since its brutality has antagonized the population. By contrast, the Catholics in Northern Ireland, where legal economic opportunities were far greater than in Afghanistan, objected to the participation of the Provisional Irish Republican Army (PIRA) in drug distribution. The resulting loss of legitimacy ultimately led PIRA to abandon its participation in the drug trade.[13]

The *character of the illicit economy* determines the extent to which it provides employment for the population. Labour-intensive illicit activities, such as the cultivation of banned crops, easily employ hundreds of thousands to millions of people in a particular locale. The smuggling of drugs or other contraband, by contrast, are labour-non-intensive illicit activities that frequently employ only hundreds of people. Belligerents' sponsorship of labour-intensive illicit economies thus brings them much greater and more widespread political capital than their sponsorship of labour-non-intensive ones. The Taliban's regulation of the labour-non-intensive illicit smuggling of licit goods bought it the favour of Afghanistan's trafficking groups in the early 1990s, but it was only in late 1995 when the Taliban came to tolerate and regulate the labour-intensive opium economy that it obtained political capital from the larger population.

The *presence or absence of independent traffickers* determines the extent to which belligerents can provide protection and regulation for the population against the traffickers. To the extent that independent traffickers are present and abuse the population, the belligerents can insert themselves into the relationship and act as protection and regulation agents, thus increasing the well-being of the population and their own political capital. If traffickers are not present, perhaps because the belligerents eliminated them, belligerents cannot provide the same scope of protection and regulation services to the producers, and hence their political capital decreases. During the 1980s and early 1990s, for example, the FARC bargained on behalf of farmers for better prices from the traffickers, and limited the abuses by the traffickers against the population. Its actions were met with widespread approval from the *cocaleros*.[14] During the late 1990s, however, the FARC displaced independent traffickers from the territories it controlled, demanded a monopoly on the sale of coca leaf, and set a ceiling on the price paid to the *cocaleros*. Consequently, the FARC's political capital plummeted substantially, further contributing to the deterioration of its legitimacy, which already was in decline as a result of its brutality and its failure to protect the population from the paramilitaries' massacres. In fact, some *cocaleros*, such as those in the Nariño region, have complained that they would prefer that the FARC were absent, since it interferes with their drug cultivation and profits by demanding a monopoly on sales of coca leaf and paste.[15]

Finally, the *government response to the illicit economy* critically influences the extent of the political capital belligerents can derive from it. The government's response can range from suppression—eradication and interdiction—to laissez faire, to some form of official sanctioning of the illegal economy, including its full-blown legalisation. Although suppression policies often dominate government responses, increasingly various less punitive policies are being explored as well. Legalisation or licensing has been adopted in the case of gems, such as in the case of diamonds in Africa under the so-called Kimberly certification process. Similarly, although easily evaded and falsified, certification systems are to distinguish illegally-sourced, processed, and transhipped timber from legally-certified wood.[16] The Organisation of American States (OAS) has called for the consideration of legalising marijuana,[17] in August 2013 Uruguay became the first country ever to fully legalise the cultivation and sale of marijuana, and Guatemala's President Otto Pérez Molina even suggested that drug trafficking in cocaine and heroin might be legalised as well.

The more the government attempts to suppress the illicit economy, the more it boosts demand for the belligerents' protection and regulation services, and the more dependent both the criminal business elites and the wider population are on the belligerents for the preservation of the illicit economy. Government suppression policies, such as the effort to eradicate illicit crops, thus frequently have the inadvertent effect of strengthening the belligerents politically by undermining the willingness of the population to provide intelligence on them to the government. Accurate and actionable human intelligence is of course essential for successful counterterrorism and counterinsurgency operations.

Although they frequently alienate the population, government efforts to crack down against illicit economies rarely result in a substantial curtailing of the belligerents' financial income. Drug eradication policies so far, for example, have not bankrupted or seriously weakened any belligerent group.[18] They tend to fail because belligerents and producers of the illicit products and services have a variety of adaptive methods at their disposal: relocating production to new areas, altering production methods to avoid detection or survive suppression, or even switching to other illegal activities. Going after the belligerents' finances, including those derived from illicit economies, is inherently difficult and rarely limits their physical resources. But in the case of labour-intensive illicit economies in poor countries, such suppression efforts, especially those that affect the larger population, can greatly increase the belligerents' political capital and hamper the government's intelligence acquisition, and hence the overall counterinsurgency and counterterrorism efforts.

Although illicit economies threaten states in a multitude of ways, and although they frequently thrive in ungoverned spaces, criminal actors with vested interests in the illicit economy frequently do not desire a complete collapse of the state. This is especially the case if there are no belligerents ready to provide the governing function and the crime entrepreneurs themselves are unable or unwilling to provide it. Nor do the criminal business elites necessarily desire a weak state, as long as the state is not antagonistic to the illicit economy. In fact, if the state is at minimum not attempting to suppress the illicit economy or is in fact favourably disposed to its existence, traffickers and producers may even support the state and oppose the belligerents. When eradication policies were suspended in Peru in 1989, for example, both the traffickers and the larger population were willing to provide critical information on the Shining Path to the military, so that the military was able to deliver fatal blows to the insurgents in the Upper Huallaga Valley.[19]

CRIME AND STATE: THE MYTHS OF INNOCENCE AND ANTAGONISM

But states do not merely acquiesce to illicit economies. They also outright often collaborate with organized crime, exploit illicit economies, and appropriate criminal groups and networks for the prosecution of military conflict or for outsourcing rule of territories they do not want to or do not have the capacity to govern. Instead of criminal elites always existing in a fully antagonistic relationship with the state, criminal organisations and the governing elites often develop a mutually beneficial accommodation. Crime can be both a convenient excuse for elites to maintain exclusionary control over political and economic access as well as a means of accomplishing both. Thus under some circumstances—and hardly only rare ones—crime can be a method of governance, sanctioned or tolerated by official political elites.

Examples abound. They include Myanmar where the junta and Burmese state were for years funded by former insurgents and drug traffickers the military had previously fought; Jamaica, or Rio de Janeiro in Brazil, where for decades governments outsourced the management of poor slums to criminal gangs, or Mexico where the ruling party for years maintained a similar corporatist relationship with drug trafficking groups as with the rest of society.[20] For decades in places such as Indonesia, Nepal, and India, ruling local or national elites have used criminal gangs for ruling and administering localities, intimidating and eliminating political opponents, and extracting votes and rents.[21]

Such an accommodation between the state and elites and criminal groups is not optimal from the perspective of the society and certainly undermines rule of law and democracy. But it may well result in a sustainable internal modus operandi, at least to the extent that external actors do not threaten such an accommodation by insisting on the destruction of the illicit economy or anti-corruption measures. Yet such outside policy measures, while disruptive, often have only cosmetic effects, for such *hybrid governance* may well involve deeply entrenched groups highly organic to local institutional and cultural settings and impossible to root out unless the outside intervener sets out to fundamentally redesign basic political arrangements and has the time, resources, and wherewithal to see such a state-remaking project through.

Nor is there always a strong social opprobrium toward the penetration of crime into politics or the appropriation of crime for state purposes. Sometimes, society mobilises against such linkages, such as in Colombia when the parapolitics scandal broke out in the middle of the 2000 decade, revealing that at least a third of the Colombian congress was connected to the vicious paramilitaries and that many municipal governments were extorted or under their thumb.[22] Yet other times, having a criminal record can give one a political advantage. Not only are politicians with known serious criminal records regularly elected in substantial numbers into India's parliament. In 2014, 34% of elected MPs of the lower chamber, the Lok Sabha, disclosed indictments for murder, attempted murder, kidnapping, provoking communal disharmony, or crimes against women, up from 30% in 2009.[23] But the criminally blemished also tend to perform much better than politicians with a clean record, perhaps because they are seen as better capable of getting things done and having better access to patronage resources by voters than politicians without criminal indictments. A candidate with a criminal record had a 13% chance of winning in the 2014 elections whereas a MP aspirant without a criminal record had only a 5% chance of winning.[24]

Indeed, despite the profound effects intense organized crime and large-scale illicit economies can have on the state and society, it is a common misconception to assume that when the drug trade or other organized-crime rackets arrive in a new place they encounter innocent virgin land with no experience in illegality or rent extraction. Sometimes that may be the case, such as when illegal loggers for the first time encounter indigenous groups in the Brazilian Amazon that have had no previous exposure to civilisation. But in all other cases, both the state and the society have pre-existing susceptibility, proclivity, and resilience to particular criminal rackets, crime-state political arrangements, and their local perturbations. The local institutional and cultural context matters a great deal in how organized crime will be able to penetrate and threaten state and society and what shape it will take.

West Africa provides an example. It has become very much the focus of international attention because of its recent drug trade epidemic in the 2000s[25] and the connections between various illicit economies and militancy and terrorism. Thus it became a favourite factoid to emphasize that al-Qaeda in the Islamic Maghreb (AQIM) leader Mokhtar Belmokhtar long smuggled cigarettes and other addictive substances in West Africa and the Maghreb, making him the poster boy of 'narco-jihadism'; or similarly, to ascribe the collapse of the Mali military in the face of jihadi militancy and Tuareg separatism to its having been hollowed out by the drug trade.[26] And of course, the region is rife with many illicit economies: whether cars and bicycles stolen in Europe and smuggled into the region, cannabis from and cocaine via Morocco heading into Europe, Viagra pills smuggled into Egypt,[27] weapons pouring out of Libya into Mali, Niger, Syria, and Nigeria, or something as seemingly harmless as eggs being smuggled in large quantities out of Tunisia. Many of these illicit enterprises, even potentially the smuggled eggs, do pose the very serious and multiple threats outlined above, even as few talk of egg-terrorism.

Yet to simply equate West Africa's chronic instability and the Maghreb's current turmoil with the recent drug trade epidemic in the area and its newly visible illicit economies fundamentally misses the deep structural roots of the problem and often leads to inadequate and even counterproductive policy recommendations. Europe's new taste for cocaine, the decline of the cocaine market in the United States, and US interdiction pressure in the Americas all helped reroute drug smuggling into West Africa. However, it was the pre-existing institutional and governance deficiencies in the region that resulted in the newly-arrived drug trade being such a potent amplifier of political instability and militancy.

Political contestation in West Africa has long focused on taking over the state to capture rents, decades before Latin American drug traffickers started using West Africa to smuggle cocaine to Europe. Indeed, almost immediately after its independence (and often predating it), the region has been characterised by a variety of illicit economies and their deep integration into the political arrangements and frameworks of the countries in the region. Such rent-generating legal, semi-illegal, or outright illegal economies have included diamonds (Sierra Leone, Liberia), gold and other precious metals, stones, and timber (Liberia, and Sierra Leone), the extraction, monopolisation, and smuggling of agricultural goods, such as cacao (Cote d'Ivoire), trafficking in humans for sexual exploitation and domestic slavery (Mali, Togo, Ghana), oil (Nigeria), and fishing (often conducted illegally and destructively by international fleets from outside West Africa).[28] Illicit diamond mining—frequently linked to politicians and tribal chiefs in Liberia—vexed the departing British colonial officers as early as the 1950s.[29] Contestation over rents from these economies fuelled much of the fighting in Sierra Leone in the 1990s and early 2000s, for example— giving rise to the concept of 'greed' wars, supposedly not motivated by political grievances, but mainly by economic interests. In this conceptualisation of violent conflict, the distinction between insurgents and criminal actors becomes highly blurred.[30]

Politics in West Africa has for decades been about taking over the state in order to control the main sources of revenue—licit or illicit. In essence, the government has been seen as a means to personal wealth, not service to the people. The state would then define (or redefine) what constitutes illegal economic behaviour and selectively issue exemptions from law enforcement and prosecution to families, friends, and its network of clients. Such political arrangements have been so pervasive in West Africa that some scholars have described the environment there as a "mafia-like bazaar, where anyone with an official designation can pillage at will (…)."[31] Moreover, fearing internal coups and yet facing little external aggression even in the context of very porous borders, many ruling elites in West

Africa after independence systematically allowed their militaries and law enforcement institutions to deteriorate. Thus, they have found themselves with institutional arrangements highly susceptible to penetration by the drug trade.[32]

In sum, the state sometimes uses and manipulates crime to its advantage. A crucial question, however, is whether the state is capable of maintaining power and control over organized crime groups or whether that power relationship reverses, with power increasingly accumulating to criminal groups, perhaps even to the point that they can dominate the relationship.[33] Originating as a pirate republic and undergoing radical institutional changes from various forms of authoritarianism to democracy, Indonesia is an example of a country where the state and political elites managed to appropriate, retain control over, and use to the state's and elite advantage criminal groups throughout the country's independent history. Even during the past two decades of democracy, political elites have not severed their linkages to organized crime but have managed to remain dominant in the power relationship.[34] In Mexico, the power of the imperial presidency and the Institutional Revolutionary Party (PRI) eventually withered as a result of economic crises, societal changes, and democratization, while the power of Mexican criminal groups increased when cocaine flows shifted to Mexico in the 1980s, resulting in the collapse of state control over organized crime. Starting in the late 1980s, the state lost the capacity to shape the behaviour of criminal groups, which began acting with increasing violence and impunity, often dictating terms to politicians and governing authorities, at least at the local level.[35] In the early 1990s Russia, the state became almost completely hollowed out, with criminal businessmen dominating and tearing apart government institutions and state functionality and organized crime groups running amok. The state that remobilises, recaptures organized crime, and recreates authoritarian rule where political power and law enforcement and intelligence authorities use organized crime, sets its terms, but also fully co-mingle with it.[36] In some ways, Vladimir Putin's Russia amounts to a *supramafia* state. There, law itself is a mechanism of expropriating private and public money for the state and elite,[37] not merely the evasion of law and the issuing of exceptions from law enforcement to one's clique as is common in places where the state functions as a mafia bazaar, such as in West Africa.

Society and Crime: As Much Predation as Dependence

At the same time, large populations around the world in areas with inadequate or problematic state presence, great poverty, and social and political marginalisation are dependent on illicit economies, including the drug trade, for economic survival and the satisfaction of other socio-economic needs. For many, participation in informal economies, if not outright illegal ones, is the only way to satisfy their human security and provide any chance of their social advancement, even as they continue to exist in a trap of insecurity, criminality, and marginalisation. The more the state is absent or deficient in the provision of legal jobs and public goods—starting with public safety and suppression of street crime and including the provision of dispute resolution mechanisms and access to justice, enforcement of contracts, and also socio-economic public goods, such as infrastructure, access to health care, and education—the more communities become susceptible to becoming dependent on and supporters of criminal entities and belligerent actors who sponsor the drug trade and other illegal economies.

By sponsoring especially labour-intensive illicit economies criminal and belligerent actors provide public goods, suboptimal as they may be.

First, they provide employment in the illegal economy. In the case of illicit crop cultivation, these job opportunities are often extensive, generating employment for hundreds of thousands, if not millions of people in particular locales. Other aspects of the drug trade, such as processing, smuggling, or the production of synthetic drugs are considerably less labour-intensive, but nonetheless generate spill-overs that often foster economic activity, such as retail. This ability to provide employment is all the more significant in places where political-economic arrangements, such as taxation systems, weak fiscal capacity, limited access to even deficient education, and monopolistic economic and political setups often fail to create jobs even at times of economic growth.

Second, both criminal entities and belligerent groups also often provide security. Of course, they are the sources of insecurity and crime in the first place, but they often regulate the level of violence, suppress street crime, such as robberies, thefts, kidnapping, and even homicides. Functioning as an order and rule provider brings criminal entities important support from the community, in addition to facilitating their illegal business since that too benefits from reduced transaction costs and increased predictability.

Organized crime groups and belligerent actors also provide dispute resolution mechanisms and even set up unofficial courts and enforce contracts—be they the *Primeiro Comando da Capital* (PCC) in Sao Paolo's shantytowns, the mafia in Sicily, or the Taliban in Afghanistan. They also provide socio-economic public goods, such as roads and health clinics. The extent to which they provide these public goods varies, of course, but their provision often takes place regardless of whether the non-state entities are politically-motivated actors or criminal enterprises. The more they do so, the more they become de facto proto-state governing entities.

In turn, such groups obtain not only large financial benefits from their participation in illegal economies, but also large political capital—support from the population and even identification of the population with these criminal and other non-state entities. Their political capital and ability to act as proto-states increase the more they transform themselves into poly-crime franchise enterprises and also acquire control of informal economies, in addition to illegal ones.

Thus, much of the debate about whether an actor is a political actor or a criminal actor is often misguided. Of course, it is critical to have a good intelligence picture and strategic understanding of a group, including its motivations, objectives, and structures, to inform the design of policy responses. For example, the effectiveness and appropriateness of suppression and negotiation strategies will vary with the strategic objectives of a group. However, even criminal organisations obtain political capital if they sponsor illicit economies and distribute patronage and public goods as a result of their sponsorship of the illicit economies in a way that outperforms the state. Moreover, most organized crime actors have at least minimal political goals, such as to influence local economic, political, law enforcement, and judicial structures in a way that it conducive to the preservation of their business. And their control of violence, corruption, and extortion on the street has profound social effects on the life of society and its ability to independently organise. High persistent levels of violence—whether they are from street crime or organized crime—eviscerate such social capital and the organisational capacity of civil society and its ability to resist organized crime.

In short, many societies and states have a deep and long history of participation in illegal enterprises and extensive criminal know-how. Over time, such illegal enterprises give rise to what I call the *technology of illegality*—networks and knowledge to evade and subvert law enforcement and transform one form of illegal economic activity into another to take advantage of new opportunities or mitigate law enforcement pressure.

In the context of poverty, limited social mobility, and political marginalisation, many may thus understand that participating in a criminal economy is illegal, but may still see such behaviour as legitimate. Thus, in addition to giving rise to a technology of illegality, long-term dependence on illicit economies for economic livelihoods and social advancement also undermines or prevents the emergence of a *culture of lawfulness*. A culture of lawfulness means that the population broadly, not every single individual, follows established rules and laws and seeks to address its grievances and disputes and obtain justice by accessing the formal legal system.[38] Where illegal actors provide public goods and illicit economies are the source of livelihoods, public goods, and social advancement, the opposite culture—*a culture of illegality*—develops. Society extolls breaking laws, evading law enforcement, and taking advantage of the state.[39] Following rules and laws is seen undesirable, foolish, and carried out only by those who lack smarts. In Medellín, Colombia, for example, I was told of a lesson mothers supposedly share with their sons: "If you make money, I'll be proud of you," a mother is reputed to say. "If you make money by tricking the law, I'll be doubly proud of you."[40] In Michoácan, Mexico, when inquiring about local population's attitudes toward the police, I was told a more drastic version of that general attitude to legality: "If a boy is smart, he'll cross the border to the United States. If he's fairly smart, he'll join the *narcos*. If he's stupid and can't do either, he'll become a policeman." Fostered by structural deficiencies, such a *culture of illegality* thus both prevents the internalisation of laws and formal rule as well as *a priori* sets up hostile relations between law enforcement officials and the population.

NOTES

1. For a comprehensive exploration of the role of illicit economies and organized crime in conflict mitigation and post-conflict reconstruction, see James Cockayne and Adam Lupel (eds.), *Peace Operations and Organized Crime: Enemies or Allies* (New York: Routledge: 2011). See also, Vanda Felbab-Brown, 'DDR in the Context of Offensive Operations, Counterterrorism, CVE and Non-Permissive Environments' and 'DDR—A Bridge Not Too Far: A Field Report from Somalia' in James Cockayne and Siobhan O'Neil (eds.), *UN DDR in an Era of Violent Extremism: Is It Fit*

for Purpose? http://cpr.unu.edu/can-the-un-demobilize-and-disengage-violent-extremists.html (New York: United Nations University, June 2015), pp. 36–61; 104–138. (New York: United Nations University, June 2015), pp. 36–61; 104–138.

2. See, for example, 'Statement by the President of the Security Council', *United Nations Security Council*, S/PRST/2010/4, 24 February 2010 and S/PRST/2009/32, 8 December 2009.

3. On the use of organized crime by Russian special operations forces, see, for example, Mark Galeotti, *Spetsnaz: Russia's Special Forces* (Oxford: Osprey Publishing, 2015). On Kremlin's use of cyber warfare by an army of trolls, see, for example, Sam Jones, 'Kremlin Alleged to Wage Cyber Warfare on Kiev', *Financial Times*, 4 June 2014; and Adrian Chen, 'The Agency', *New York Times Magazine*, 2 June 2015.

4. James Mattis and Frank Hoffman, 'Future Warfare: The Rise of Hybrid Wars', *U.S. Naval Institute Proceedings Magazine*, vol. 132, no. 11/1233, November 2005, pp. 18–19.

5. Vanda Felbab-Brown, 'The Political Economy of Illegal Domains in India and China', *International Lawyer*, vol. 43, no. 4, winter 2009, pp. 1411–1428; and Brian Martin, *The Shanghai Green Gang: Politics and Organized Crime, 1919–1937* (Berkeley, CA: University of California Press, 1996).

6. Mónica Serrano and María Celia Toro, 'From Drug Trafficking to Transnational Organized Crime in Latin America', in Mats Berdal and Monica Serrano (eds.), *Transnational Organized Crime and International Security: Business as Usual?* (Boulder: Lynne Rienner, 2002), pp. 141–154; and Mauricio Rubio, 'Violence, Organized Crime, and the Criminal Justice System in Colombia', *Journal of Economic Issues*, vol. 32, no. 2, pp. 605–610.

7. See, for example, Coletta A. Youngers and Eileen Rosin (eds.), *Drugs and Democracy in Latin America* (Boulder: Lynne Rienner, 2005).

8. For details on the economic effects of illicit economies, see, for example, Francisco E. Thoumi, *Illegal Drugs, Economy, and Society in the Andes* (Baltimore, MD: John Hopkins University Press, 2004); Pranab Bardhan, 'Corruption and Development: A Review of the Issues', *Journal of Economic Literature*, vol. 35, no. 3, 1997, pp. 1320–1365; Peter Reuter, 'The Mismeasurement of Illegal Drug Markets: The Implications of Its Irrelevance', in Susan Pozo (ed.), *Exploring the Underground Economy* (Kalamazoo, MI: W.E. Upjohn Institute, 1996), pp. 63–80; and Mauricio Reina, 'Drug Trafficking and the National Economy', in Charles Berquist, Ricardo Peñaranda, and Gonzalo Sánchez G. (eds.), *Violence in Colombia 1990–2000: Waging War and Negotiating Peace* (Wilmington, DE: A Scholarly Resources Inc. Imprint, 2001).

9. A tanker carrying 500 metric tons of European industrial waste illegally dumped its cargo in the port, killing or sickening thousands, and overwhelming the state's infrastructure. See 'The Abidjan toxic waste dump', editorial, *L'Occidental*, 4 October 2006, http://www.loccidental.net/english/spip.php?article138.

10. This section draws heavily on Vanda Felbab-Brown's book, *Shooting Up: Counterinsurgency and the War on Drugs* (Washington DC: The Brookings Institution, 2009).

11. Author's interviews in Colombia, autumn 2005.

12. See, for example, Cynthia McClintock, *Revolutionary Movements in Latin America: El Salvador's FMLN & Peru's Shining Path* (Washington DC: United States Institute of Peace Press, 1998); and Cynthia McClintock, 'The War on Drugs: The Peruvian Case', *Journal of Interamerican Studies and World Affairs*, vol. 30, no. 2 and 3, Summer/ Fall 1988, pp. 127–142.

13. Andrew Silke, 'Drink, Drugs, and Rock 'n' Roll: Financing Loyalist Terrorism in Northern Ireland—Part Two', *Studies in Conflict and Terrorism*, vol. 23, no. 2, April–June 2000, pp. 107–127.

14. See, for example, Nazih Richani, *Systems of Violence: The Political Economy of War and Peace in Colombia* (Albany, NY: State University of New York Press, 2002); and Francisco Gutiérrez Sanín, 'Criminal Rebels? A Discussion of Civil War and Criminality from the Colombian Experience', *Politics and Society*, vol. 32, no. 2, June 2004, pp. 257–285.

15. Author's interviews with Colombian and U.S. government officials, Bogotá, Colombia, November 2005, and Washington DC, Spring and Summer 2007, Summer and Autumn 2009, and Spring 2015.

16. Vanda Felbab-Brown, 'Indonesia Field Report III: The Orangutan's Road: Illegal Logging, and Mining in Indonesia', *The Brookings Institution*, February 2013.

17. 'The Drug Problem in the Americas', *Organization of American States*, 2013, http://www.oas.org/documents/eng/press/Introduction_and_Analytical_Report.pdf; and 'Scenarios for the Drug Problem in the Americas 2013–2025', *Organization of American States*, 2013, http://www.oas.org/documents/eng/press/Scenarios_Report.PDF.

18. A 2007 classified White House study estimated that the FARC's drug income fell between 2003 and 2005 by a third and it was now between $60 and $115 million a year. Author's interviews with U.S. government officials, Washington DC, spring 2007. See Juan Forero, 'Colombia's Low-Tech Coca Assault', *Washington Post*, 7 July 2007. Even disregarding the notorious difficulties in estimating profits from illicit economies, the estimates betray the extraordinary difficulty of trying to bankrupt belligerent groups by eradication. If six years of the largest aerial spraying campaign

ever, Plan Colombia, managed to reduce the FARC's income only to a still extraordinarily high $60 million a year (the lower bound of the estimate), the prospects are not good that such efforts will be successful elsewhere. Indeed, bankrupting belligerents via the eradication of illicit crops from which they profit has yet to work anywhere.

19. José E. Gonzales, 'Guerrillas and Coca in the Upper Huallaga Valley', in David Scott Palmer (ed.), *Shining Path of Peru* (New York: St. Martin's Press, 1994), pp. 123–144.

20. See, for example, Bertil Lintner, 'Drugs and Economic Growth: Ethnicity and Exports' in Robert I. Rotberg (ed.), *Burma: Prospect for a Democratic Future* (Washington DC: Brookings Institution Press, 1998), pp. 165–184; Enrique Desmond Arias, 'The Impact of Organized Crime on Governance: A Desk Study of Jamaica', in Camino Kavanagh (ed.), *Getting Smart and Scaling Up: Impact of Organized Crime on Governance in Developing Countries*, (Center for International Cooperation, NYU, June 2013), http://cic.nyu.edu/sites/default/files/kavanagh_crime_developing_countries_report_w_annexes.pdf; and Enrique Desmond Arias and Corinne Davis Rodrigues, 'The Myth of Personal Security: Criminal Gangs, Dispute Resolution, and Identity in Rio de Janeiro's Favelas', *Latin American Politics and Society*, vol. 48, no. 4, 2006, pp. 53–81; Mónica Serrano, 'States of Violence: State-Crime Relations in Mexico', in Wil Pansters (ed.), *Violence, Coercion, and State-Making in the Twentieth-Century Mexico* (Stanford, CA: Stanford University Press, 2012), pp. 135–158; and Vanda Felbab-Brown, *Narco Noir: Mexico's Cartels, Corruption, and Security Strategies* (Washington DC: The Brookings Institution Press, 2016, forthcoming).

21. See, for example, Vanda Felbab-Brown, 'The Impact of Organized Crime on Governance: The Case Study of Nepal', in Kavanagh (ed.), *Getting Smart and Scaling Up: Impact of Organized Crime on Governance in Developing Countries*, and Vanda Felbab-Brown, *Indonesia Field Report I: Crime as a Mirror of Politics: Urban Gangs in Indonesia*, The Brookings Institution, February 2013.

22. For other examples of the penetration of crime into politics in Latin America, see *Illicit Networks and Politics in Latin America* (Stockholm and The Hague: International Idea, Netherlands Institute for Multiparty Democracy (NIMD), and Netherlands Institute of International Relations [Clingendael], 2014).

23. 'Every Third Newly-Elected MP Has Criminal Background', *Times of India*, 18 May 2014, http://timesofindia.indiatimes.com/news/Every-third-newly-elected-MP-has-criminal-background/article-show/35306963.cms.

24. Ibid.

25. See, for example, James Cockayne and Phil Williams, 'The Invisible Tide: Towards an International Strategy to Deal with Drug Trafficking Through West Africa', *International Peace Institute*, October 2009; Davin O'Regan, 'Narco-States: Africa's Next Menace', *New York Times*, 12 March 2012; Davin O'Regan and Peter Thompson, 'Advancing Stability and Reconciliation in Guinea-Bissau: Lessons from Africa's First Narco-State', *Africa Center for Strategic Studies Special Report*, June 2013, http://africacenter.org/wp-content/uploads/2013/06/SpecialReport-Guinea-Bissau-JUN2013-EN.pdf; and Neil Carrier and Gernot Klantschnig, *Africa and the War on Drugs* (Zed Books: 2012); Kwesi Aning, Sampson B. Kwarkye, and John Pokoo, 'A Case Study of Ghana', in Kavanagh (ed.), *Getting Smart and Scaling Up: Impact of Organized Crime on Governance in Developing Countries*; Summer Walker, 'A Desk Study of Sierra Leone', in Kavanagh (ed.), *Getting Smart and Scaling Up: Impact of Organized Crime on Governance in Developing Countries*.

26. For a detailed analysis of the drug trade in Mali, see, for example, Peter Tinti et al, 'Illicit Trafficking and Instability in Mali: Past, Present, and Future', *The Global Initiative against Transnational Organized Crime*, January 2014, http://www.globalinitiative.net/download/global-initiative/Global%20Initiative%20-%20Organized%20Crime%20and%20Illicit%20Trafficking%20in%20Mali%20-%20Jan%202014.pdf.

27. 'Trafficking in North Africa', *Economist,* 17 August 2013.

28. See, for example, Jean-Francois Bayart, Stephen Ellis and Beatrice Hibou, *The Criminalization of the State in Africa* (Bloomington, IN: Indiana University Press, 1999).

29. See, for example, William Reno, 'Understanding Criminality in West African Conflicts', *International Peacekeeping*, vol. 16, no, 1, February 2009, p 52.

30. See, for example, Collier Paul and Anke Hoeffler, 'Greed and Grievance in Civil Wars', *Oxford Economic Papers*, vol. 56, 2004, pp. 563–595; Michael Ross, 'What Do We Know about Natural Resources and Civil War?', *Journal of Peace Research*, vol. 31, no. 3, 2004, pp. 337–356; and Jeremy Weinstein, *Inside Rebellion The Politics of Insurgent Violence* (New York: Cambridge University Press, 2007).

31. George B.N. Ayittey, *Africa in Chaos* (New York: St. Martin's Griffin, 1999), p. 151. See also Moises Naím, 'Mafia States', *Foreign Affairs*, May/June 2012, https://www.foreignaffairs.com/articles/2012-04-20/mafia-states; and Sarah Chayes, *Thieves of State: Why Corruption Threatens Global Security* (New York: W.W. Norton, 2015).

32. For details on the role and evolution of law enforcement in West Africa to fight organized crime and belligerency, see, for example, Vanda Felbab-Brown and James J.F. Forest, 'Political Violence and the Illicit Economies

of West Africa', *Terrorism and Political Violence*, vol. 24, no. 5, November 2012, pp. 787–806.

33. For a similar classification of the types of organized crime and of militant participation in illicit economies as predatory, parasitical, or symbiotic, see R.T. Naylor, *Wages of Crime: Black Markets, Illegal Finance, and the Underworld Economy* (Ithaca, NY: Cornell University Press, 2002).

34. Author's interviews in Indonesia, autumn 2012. See also Bertil Linter, *Blood Brothers: The Criminal Underworld of Asia* (New York: Palgrave Macmillan, 2003).

35. Serrano (2012); Felbab-Brown, *Narco Noir*, (forthcoming).

36. See, Vadim Volkov, *Violent Entrepreneurs: The Use of Force in the Making of Russian Capitalism* (Cornell, NY: Cornell University Press, 2002); Mark Galeotti, 'The Mafiya and the New Russia', *Australian Journal of Politics and History*, vol. 44, no. 3, September 1998, pp. 415–429; and Mark Galeotti, 'The Russian 'Mafiya': Consolidation and Globalization', *Global Crime*, vol. 6, no, 1, 2004, pp. 54–69. For evolution of the state-organized crime relations in other post-Soviet countries, such as Ukraine and the Caucasus, see Alexander Kupatadze, *Organized Crime, Political Transitions, and State Formation in Post-Soviet Eurasia* (New York: Palgrave Macmillan, 2012).

37. Jordan Gans-Morse, 'Threats to Property Rights in Russia: From Private Coercion to State Aggression', *Post-Soviet Affairs*, vol. 28, no. 3, 2012, pp. 263–295.

38. For further details on the concept of *culture of lawfulness*, see Roy Godson, 'A Guide to Developing a Culture of Lawfulness', presentation at the Symposium on the Role of Civil Society in Countering Organized Crime: Global Implications of the Palermo, Sicily, 2000; 'Guiding Principles for Stabilization and Reconstruction' (The Web Version), *United States Institute of Peace*, Section 7.9: 'Culture of Lawfulness', http://www.usip.org/guiding-principles-stabilization-and-reconstruction-the-web-version/7-rule-law/culture-lawfulness.

39. See, for example, Francisco Thoumi, *Illegal Drugs, Economy, and Society in the Andes* (Baltimore, MD: John Hopkins University Press, 2003).

40. Author's interviews with NGO representatives and local residents in comúna 13, Medellín, January 2011.

CHAPTER 2

Organized Crime as a Threat to Sustainable Development: Understanding the Evidence

Tuesday Reitano

Abstract The chapter highlights the main arguments for a development response to organized crime, to mitigating its impact on vulnerable communities and the integrity of the state, and to building long-term resilience to countering organized crime in the future. Specifically, it discusses the evidence base of organized crime's impact vis-à-vis four core development areas: health and wellbeing, violence and conflict, governance and the rule of law, livelihoods and the environment. It concludes that experiences collected from around the globe definitely show the manifold and interconnected negative impacts of organized crime on development.

Keywords Organized crime • Development • Sustainable Development Goals

The 2030 Agenda for Sustainable Development (SDGs), the successor development framework to the Millennium Development Goals (MDGs), promulgated by the 193 member states of the United Nations in September 2015, lays out a series of transformative goals and targets that are perceived as central to achieving the United Nations' (UN) core goals of achieving peace, eradicating poverty and ensuring sustainable

T. Reitano (✉)
Global Initiative against Transnational Organized Crime, Geneva, Switzerland

© The Author(s) 2018
V. Comolli (ed.), *Organized Crime and Illicit Trade*,
https://doi.org/10.1007/978-3-319-72968-8_2

23

development for all peoples.[1] Countering organized crime is explicitly referenced as a critical target in Goal 16, but the repeated mentions across the document of organized crime's many manifestations—from forced labour to wildlife trafficking—evidence the fact that organized crime has become a far reaching, pernicious threat that is now central to the mandate of development actors. In a recent study, the Global Initiative against Transnational Organized Crime found that of the 169 targets included in that framework, 23 of them—12.5% of the total—will require directly addressing a criminal flow or network in order to be achieved.[2] The primary onus for the achievement of the SDGs is at national level, and it is therefore imperative that national policymakers have the capacity to identify, understand and respond to the impact of organized crime as a development challenge.

Addressing organized crime is a challenge for all states, regardless of size, capacity or income level. The negative impacts of organized crime on development are manifold and diverse, and while development practitioners prefer evidence-based programming, the evidence basis on the relationship between organized crime and development has still not been fully expounded. The organized crime narrative is not easily translated to the mainstream development community, and the goal of this chapter is to provide the evidence based foundation of why and how organized crime impacts on the main sectors of development: on violence and conflict; stability and security; governance and the rule of law; livelihoods and the environment, and on health and well-being.

Organized Crime as a Development Issue: Evidence Basis and Evolution

Health and Well-Being

Public health is the area where the discourse around organized crime and development is perhaps the most advanced. This was driven by the causal relationship identified between injecting drug use and HIV/AIDS transmission: the World Health Organisation (WHO) estimates that one in every ten new HIV infections globally is as a result of injecting drug use, and in some regions of Eastern Europe and Central Asia this rises to as high as 80% of all new infections.[3] The negative spill-over effects of drug trafficking in high transit zones has been well documented. The common practice by trafficking groups of using the drugs themselves as a means of paying for services has resulted in higher local consumption along major routes in the Americas, the Caribbean and in Africa. The subsequent costs of responding to illicit drug use and high-levels of drug addiction is considerable, for governments, communities and individuals, both financially and socially, and has arguably weighed heaviest on society's most vulnerable. High levels of illicit drug use are associated with reduced confidence in public health institutions, restricted access to health services and medicinal drugs in those populations, and with rising levels of crime and violence.

For the past two decades, responses to the paradigm have been largely driven by criminal justice approaches—the infamous 'War on Drugs'— that criminalised both drug trafficking and use.[4] The evidence that this has arguably done more harm than good, whilst having little appreciable impact on global drug markets, has led to a shift in prevailing international policy that is development led.[5] This being said, however, there remains considerable uncertainty as to what a development or public health approach to drugs might look like, particularly in some countries where it is most urgently required given their lack of infrastructure and funds.[6] Much energy is focused on questions of decriminalisation and legalisation, though early experiments in this area have shown that it is no silver bullet, and that the impacts on the consumption of other drugs, and on illicit markets in neighbouring jurisdictions also need to be considered.[7]

The drug debate has dominated the discussions around organized crime as an issue for the health sector, arguably to the neglect of other public health issues that would warrant similar levels of concern. The growing prevalence of counterfeit medicines in the developing world, for example, is a burgeoning illicit industry for which neither a reliable evidence basis nor effective responses have been developed. From as far back as 1988, the World Health Assembly has had resolutions targeted at the prevention and detection of the export, import and smuggling of counterfeit pharmaceutical products,[8] yet the problem has proliferated almost unfettered. Some estimates have suggested that as much as 60% or more of medicine in certain vulnerable countries might be falsified, and estimates of the value of the illicit trade run into billions annually. The long-term impact is that counterfeit medicines erode public confidence in health institutions, with critical implications during large-scale crises such as the Ebola outbreak in 2013, undermine human health and security, and risk the growth of resistant strains of key viral diseases such as malaria.[9] Yet, despite this, within the SDG goals for health, ensuring safe access to appropriate and integral medication was framed as an issue to be addressed within the framework of intellectual property, rather than criminality and integrity. The challenge of fraudulent or substandard fertilisers or compromised seed banks was handled similarly within the agriculture sector.

An additional issue, the illicit trade in tobacco products, has a major impact on public health. It is said to increase the number of smokers, daily consumption rates and pose health risks due to sub-standard or dangerous materials being used.[10] It provides an additional threat to development, however, as notorious armed groups the world over, including Hezbollah, al-Qaeda in the Islamic Maghreb (AQIM) and the Kurdistan Workers' Party (PKK), have funded or continue to fund their activities through the sale of illicit tobacco.[11] The impact of conflict and violence on development are considerable and protracted, as the subsequent section will demonstrate.

Violence and Conflict

The use of violence is one of the defining features of an organized crime group, used for intimidation, extortion and as a criminal service in its own right, and as such, organized crime has become on the of leading drivers of violence, insecurity and conflict. In 2005, the report of the UN Secretary-General, *In Larger Freedom*, highlighted organized crime as one of the principle threats to peace and security in the twenty-first century.[12] The *2011 World Development Report* calculated that areas exposed to prolonged violence and conflict experienced a 20% loss in development performance in comparison to more stable and peaceful peers.[13] The *2015 States of Fragility* report released by the Organisation for Economic Co-operation and Development (OECD), which uses a multi-dimensional framework to measure state fragility, demonstrated clearly that transnational threats such as organized crime and terrorism have served as a leveller across states, negatively affecting high income, middle income and lower income states equally, and demanding shared responses and shared responsibility to control the flows and mitigate the impact.[14]

Discussions around the relationship of organized crime to violence and conflict sit at the nexus of two debates: between gang violence and drug trafficking in the Americas, regions posting the highest levels of homicide globally; and in the context of weak, failing or failed states where the interwoven connections between conflict actors, resources, illicit flows and insurgencies have been prominently explored.

The United Nations Office on Drugs and Crime (UNODC) Homicide Report published in 2014 found that of the half a million people who are killed each year as result of intentional homicidal violence, organized crime is a significant cause. In Central America and Mexico, which suffer from the world's highest homicide rates, 30% of murders are related to organized crime or gang violence. The operation of illicit drug markets drives violence and homicide levels, often due to violent competition between rival groups or involved parties, and the psycho-pharmacological effects of using certain drugs, such as cocaine and amphetamines, are also proven to have been causally linked to violence,[15] such that in Latin America, rates of violent crime are six times higher than in the rest of the world.[16] Rapid urbanisation and sharp income inequalities across the globe, but particularly in the southern hemisphere, have resulted in slums characterised by high crime, violence and insecurity. Neglect of organized crime's ability to penetrate vulnerable urban environments carries high risks, for which Cape Town is a case in point: the city has the highest rates of murder and drug related crime on the continent, with murders at a rate of nearly seven per day.[17]

An excessive focus on drug trafficking, however, neglects that rarely are criminal groups exclusively involved in just drug markets. A contemporary feature of organized crime is that groups are frequently poly-crime groups, engaging in a gamut of activities in addition to drug trafficking, including piracy, smuggling of migrants, smuggling of body parts, trade in artefacts, arms trade, extortion, kidnapping, prostitution, illegal mining and illegal logging. Therefore in the increasingly complicated debates around the utility of drug legalisation, opponents argue that it would not by itself lead to the reduction of violence. Using security and justice-based interventions to interrupt, interdict and seize drug revenues away from organized crime groups may significantly weaken them, and in some cases could potentially lead to their vanishing altogether, but in the majority of cases it would still require addressing of the other forms of criminal revenue that might continue to fuel the groups. It further neglects that violence is perpetuated by groups involved in other forms of illicit activity, and more importantly, by the market for criminal protection itself. Competition between criminal groups over routes and markets is a significant source of violence across industries, and the use of violence or the threat thereof is also a means of generating income. Protection and extortion are in themselves defining features of territorially-based mafia groups across the globe.[18]

Vice-versa, efforts that have focused on the manifestations of violence and conflict without assessing the role of illicit flows and criminal networks as causal factors have similarly been unsuccessful. For example, analysis of experimentation with gang truces, including those most recently in the Americas between 2012–14, showed that the most successful of these achieved their primary objective to reduce the rate of violent homicides in the short term, but in the medium to long term they were challenged to achieve sustainability whilst trafficking activities continued.[19] Furthermore, the focus on one metric—homicides—as the primary indicator of success or failure, overlooked the fact that during the period of truces organized criminal activity, extortions and other violent crime rose exponentially.[20]

In the context of failed and failing states, the analysis around the role of illicit resources flows has been quite widely examined, particularly in the context of Africa and the post-colonial *Congo wars* in Central and West Africa. In these discussions, violent protection of access to natural resources such as minerals, oil and wildlife, have been shown to be linked to the cause, exacerbation and protraction of conflict.[21] In more recent conflicts in the Sahel and Libya starting in 2012, similar analysis has been applied to illicit trafficking in drugs, the smuggling of migrants and other criminal transit flows as serving as a means of resourcing insurgencies.[22] However, in both cases, the failure of internationally sponsored peace and transition processes to adequately address illicit flows and provide effective means to separate criminal activity from legitimate grievance, and to protect the institutions of the state from penetration of illicit flows, has become widely cited as reasons for the resurgence of conflict and subsequent state failure.[23]

The ability of the international community to respond to the threat of organized crime has been significantly hampered by the strong emphasis placed on the issue as a *security* threat, which results in overly militarised, security-driven responses that have the tendency to lead to the escalation rather than suppression of violence,[24] the entrenchment of insurgencies and has been attributed by some as a driver of growing trends in violent extremism in a diverse range of theatres. Therefore, the need to work towards genuinely integrated strategies, or even development lead approaches, has become a priority. Some cite the work done to reduce crime and violence in the *favelas* in Brazil, and to reinstitute the state as a meaningful entity, as a good practice in this regard,[25] but achieving this level of intervention would arguably be a challenge in those states with lower capacity and less resources.

Governance and the Rule of Law

The inclusion of goals and targets around governance and the rule of into the SDGs is a seismic shift from their predecessors, the MDGs. For the first time, this compelling development agenda recognises a set of drivers relating to governance, social justice and the rule of law are fundamental to ensuring development and human security. Organized crime, and the corruption and impunity that result from its practice and perpetuation, threatens the legitimacy of the social contract, undermines the rule of law and slows, if not reverses, development progress.

Political and public sector corruption has allowed organized crime to develop or flourish, undermining the legitimacy of state institutions, and providing limited incentives for citizens not to engage in, or benefit from, organized crime.[26] International concern around electoral integrity has shifted from the threat of elections captured by violence, towards concern for the infiltration of illicit funds generated by organized crime buying seats, candidates and elections themselves.[27] It is increasingly recognised that for criminal groups, corruption can be both a means to an end, but also an end in itself, which leads to state actors profiting from, engaging in and protecting criminal behaviour, and working in complicity with criminal networks rather than in the interests of the population.[28]

However, while it is often said that organized crime has 'infiltrated' politics, often the complicity is a two-way street, and that politicians have strategically chosen to ally with criminal groups to advance their own ends. In a number of countries, the use of organized crime to perpetuate politically motivated violence—assassinations, disappearances, strategically targeted violence—have done considerable damage to the credibility of the state and political parties, as well as of local government.[29] There are furthermore numerous examples in which states choose to reach an accommodation with criminal groups over control of territory or illicit markets, either because they cannot or are unwilling to attempt to exert state control and service delivery in those areas. These 'pax Mafioso' style agreements give the opportunity for criminal groups to build their legitimacy with local populations, and strengthen their positions.[30]

The long-term impact of the intertwining of crime and politics is serious. Democratic governance and integrity are arguably the cornerstones of effective and sustainable conflict prevention and resolution, respect for basic human rights and fundamental freedoms, and the preservation and advancement of equal social and political rights, all of which arguably serve as the foundations for sustainable development. Addressing this, however, is a significant challenge and requires a sharpening of the range of instruments tailored to counter corruption with a specific focus on the role of criminal groups. While criminal justice and law enforcement approaches will continue to be imperative for responding to organized crime, they become hamstrung in the face of institutionalised or widespread corruption. As a consequence, development actors have an important role in addressing weaknesses identified in the broader governance framework, identifying and prioritising organized crime actors and activities that do most harm in a given context, and ensuring that citizen needs and respect for fundamental human rights are central to proposed remedies.[31] Furthermore, as the subsequent section will show, the legitimacy and currency upon which criminal groups often trade, is their ability to offer advantageous livelihoods. The role of development actors in providing viable, legitimate and sustainable livelihood alternatives is a critical component of any strategy seeking to counter organized crime's impact on governance and the rule of law.

Livelihoods and the Environment

The natural environment is the primary global source of livelihoods, and is thus a critical resource for human survival and development. While of course the environment has intrinsic value in its own right, these concepts are interwoven in this analysis, because of their linkages and interdependence.

There is plentiful evidence of the harm that organized crime wreaks on the environment. Key species such as tigers, elephants and rhinos have been driven to the point of extinction by criminal networks poaching animals for sale on global black markets. In illegal mining, logging, fishing and oil theft, finite natural resources are pillaged at unsustainable rates and by means that are not safe for the eco systems from which they come, nor for those that are often coerced into facilitating the trade. At the same time, through its criminal practices, organized crime can do serious environmental damage, such as unsafe disposal of toxic waste dumping, or trafficking in ozone depleting substances.[32] Even those crimes without direct linkages to the environment have proven detrimental: a 2014 study showed that drug trafficking is contributing significantly to deforestation in the Amazon.[33]

The primary motivating factor for those involved in organized crime is to garner profit, and of the reasons that organized crime groups can flourish and develop legitimacy is in those areas where illicit trafficking or other forms of criminal behaviour provide the best possible livelihoods for the local populations. It is largely the case that, whilst plying their illicit trade, organized crime groups not only degrade the sustainable livelihood alternatives of the population, but also undermine legitimate markets and economic opportunity with unfair competition, protectionism and corruption. This thereby creates a vicious cycle where engaging in criminal behaviour increasingly becomes the only viable option.

The development sector can emphasise large-scale reforms to health and education systems in developing countries, but oftentimes what matters most to people on a day-to-day level are more basic issues like having an income and feeling secure in their neighbourhood. Therefore, whoever can deliver these fundamental daily societal needs, will gain legitimacy with local populations. Again, if states are unable to provide the specific services that communities prioritise, then the window of opportunity for criminal exploitation is opened even more widely. This is not only relevant in contexts of labour intensive illicit economies, but also those where the delivery of key services has become hybridised or privatised, offering additional prospects for rent-seeking and unjust distribution.[34]

The example is well illustrated by looking at the criminal practice of illegal, unregulated and unreported (IUU) fishing in West Africa. The Gulf of Guinea is home to one of the world's most resource rich marine environments, and is also estimated to have the highest level of IUU fishing on earth. West African coastal states are losing 37% of their annual catch to IUU fishing, estimated at US$ 1.3 billion annually, mainly to foreign fishing trawlers operating under flags of convenience, with most of the illegally-caught fish is taken to the European Union (EU) and China, the world's biggest fish markets. Industrial overfishing is destroying the livelihoods and food security of some of the world's poorest people, forcing them to seek new alternatives. The loss of fishing livelihoods has been attributed to the rise of maritime piracy in the Gulf of Guinea, to the attraction of local fisherman to engage in drug trafficking and to facilitate other forms of organized crime.[35] The collapse of local fish stocks in Senegal in 2005 has been attributed as a trigger for a migrant crisis in 2006, where more than 40,000 attempted to migrate illegally to Europe, with more than 6,000 estimated to have lost their lives.[36]

This story of the illicit pillaging of environmental resource replacing legitimate livelihoods with criminal ones also underpins the rise of piracy off the coast of Somalia, and the complicity of local communities in the Southern Africa wildlife poaching crisis has traded short term returns against the long-term diversity of their ecosystems.[37] In Afghanistan, poppy may be a less lucrative crop than the country's famous fruit trees, but it serves as a resilience strategy in times of drought, and the traffickers offer access to credit that neither the government nor the legitimate financial sector would do within the fragile agricultural economy.[38]

Lack of legitimate livelihoods increases the vulnerability of people, making them more susceptible to engaging in criminal enterprises, and of falling victim to organized crime. This has been shown to be true across the human trafficking industry, from forced labour to sexual exploitation.[39] This paradigm is compounded where a corrupt system operating with impunity does little to censure criminal acts.

In these contexts the challenge is complex to address, as if a response is to be sustainable it requires simultaneously protecting or recovering the environment from the damage wrought, combatting the illicit trade itself and breaking down the legitimacy that criminal groups have gained through the provision of livelihoods, and finding alternative livelihoods for those involved in the trade. In both the latter two cases, these are quintessentially development challenges, but ones that need to be specifically re-orientated to help communities escape from this vicious cycle that has been described as a 'crime trap'.[40]

The evidence discussed above highlights the many ways in which organized crime undermines development, encompassing governance, health, environmental and security issues. Crucially, the experiences collected from around the globe make it impossible to ignore the interconnectedness of the impacts of the phenomenon and the domino effect transnational organized crime gives rise to. The link among cigarette smuggling, revenue loss, health problems and terrorism funding is particularly telling in this respect. Furthermore, it lays the ground for ensuing chapters: security approaches are not always the most effective or desirable solutions to problems that have such broad ranging implications.

Notes

1. 'Transforming our World: The 2030 Agenda for Sustainable Development', *United Nations (UN)* (New York: United Nations, 2015).
2. 'Organised Crime: a cross-cutting threat to sustainable development', *Global Initiative against Transnational Organized Crime* (Geneva: Global Initiative against Transnational Organized Crime, 2015).
3. 'Technical Guide for Countries to Set Targets for Universal Access to HIV Prevention, Treatment and Care for Injecting Drug Users', *World Health Organization (WHO), United Nations Office on Drugs and Crime (UNOCD) and UNAIDS* (Geneva: WHO, 2013).
4. Catherine Martin, *Casualties of War: How the War on Drugs is harming the world's poorest* (London: Health Poverty Action, 2015).
5. 'Taking Control: Pathways to drug policies that work', *Global Commission on Drug Policy* (Global Commission on Drug Policy, 2014).
6. 'Report on the Drug Problem in the Americas', *Organization of American States (OAS)* (Cartagena: Organization of American States, 2013); 'Not Just in Transit: Drugs, the State and Society in West Africa', *West Africa Commission on Drugs (WACD)* (Geneva: West Africa Commission on Drugs, 2014).
7. Kellen Russoniello, 'The Devil (and Drugs) in the Details: Portugal's Focus on Public Health as a Model for Decriminalization of Drugs in Mexico', *Yale Journal of Health Policy, Law and Ethics,* vol. 12, no. 2, 2013, art. 4; 'New frontiers or old boundaries? Reconsidering Approaches to the Security and Development Nexus in the Context of Responses to Organized Crime, Conflict, and Insurgency', *Global Initiative against Transnational Organized Crime* (Geneva: Global Initiative against Transnational Organized Crime, 2015).
8. 'Guidelines for the development of measures to counter counterfeit drugs', *WHO* (Geneva: WHO, 1999).
9. 'Organized Crime: A Cross-Cutting Threat to Sustainable Development', *Global Initiative against Transnational Organized Crime,* January 2015.
10. Ibid.
11. Louise Shelley and Sharon Malzer, 'The Nexus of Organized Crime and Terrorism: Two Case Studies in Cigarette Smuggling', *International*

Journal of Comparative and Applied Criminal Justice, vol. 32, no. 1, Spring 2008, pp. 43–63.

12. 'In Larger Freedom: towards development, security and human rights for all', *UN General Assembly* (New York: United Nations, 2005).

13. 'World Development Report 2011', *World Bank* (Washington, DC: World Bank, 2011).

14. 'States of Fragility 2015: Meeting Post-2015 Ambitions', *Organisation for Economic Co-operation and Development (OECD)* (Paris: OECD Publishing, 2015).

15. 'Homicide Report 2013', *UNODC* (Vienna: United Nations, 2014).

16. Vanda Felbab-Brown, *Bringing the State to the Slum: confronting organised crime and urban violence in Latin America* (Washington, DC: Brookings, 2011).

17. 'Organized Crime: A Cross-Cutting Threat to Sustainable Development'.

18. Stephen Ellis and Mark Shaw, 'Does Organised Crime Exist in Africa?', *African Affairs*, vol. 115, no. 457, September 2015.

19. Charles M. Katz and Luis Enrique Amaya, *The Gang Truce as a Form of Violence Intervention: Implications for Policy and Practice* (San Salvador: SolucionES, 2015).

20. Mabel Gonzalez-Bustelo, 'El-Salvador's Gang Truce: a lost opportunity?', *Open Democracy*, 18 May 2015, https://www.opendemocracy.net/opensecurity/mabel-gonz%C3%A1lez-bustelo/el-salvador%E2%80%99s-gang-truce-lost-opportunity.

21. Mark Shaw and Tuesday Reitano. *The Evolution of Organised Crime in Africa: towards a new response* (Pretoria: Institute for Security Studies, 2013); Laura Freeman, *Breaking the Chain: Can sanctions crack the connections between organised crime and insurgency?* (Geneva: Global Initiative against Transnational Organized Crime, 2016).

22. Tuesday Reitano and Mark Shaw, *Fixing a fractured state: breaking the cycles of crime, corruption and conflict in Mali and the Sahel* (Geneva: Global Initiative against Transnational Organized Crime, 2015).

23. Stewart Patrick, *Weak Links: fragile states, global threats and international security* (Oxford: Oxford University Press, 2011).

24. 'Report on the Drug Problem in the Americas'.

25. 'Bringing the state back into the favelas of Rio de Janeiro: understanding changes in community life after the UPP pacification process', *World Bank* (Washington, DC: World Bank, 2012).

26. Camino Kavanagh, *Getting Smart and Scaling Up: Responding to the Impact of Organized Crime on Governance in Developing Countries* (New York: Centre for International Cooperation, 2013).

27. Global Commission on Elections, Democracy and Security, *Deepening Democracy: A Strategy for Improving the Integrity of Elections Worldwide*

(Stockholm / Geneva: International Institute for Democracy and Electoral Assistance (International IDEA) / Kofi Annan Foundation, 2012); 'Illicit Networks and Politics in Latin America', *International IDEA* (Stockholm: International IDEA, 2014).

28. Sarah Chayes, *Thieves of State: why corruption threatens global security* (New York: W.W. Norton & Co., 2015); Tom Burgis, *The Looting Machine: Warlords, tycoons, smugglers and the systematic theft of Africa's wealth* (London: William Collins, 2015); Moisés Naím, 'Mafia States: Organised Crime takes Office', *Foreign Affairs*, May/June2012.

29. 'Illicit Networks and Politics in Latin America'.

30. Tuesday Reitano and Marcena Hunter, *Organised Crime and Service Delivery* (Stockholm: International IDEA, 2016); Kavanagh, *Getting Smart and Scaling Up*.

31. Kavanagh, *Getting Smart and Scaling Up: Responding to the Impact of Organized Crime on Governance on Developing Countries*

32. Justin Gosling, *The Global Response to Transnational Organized Environmental Crime* (Geneva: Global Initiative against Transnational Organised Crime, 2014).

33. Brian Clark Howard, 'Drug Trafficking Poses Surprising Threats to Rain Forests, Scientists Find', *National Geographic*, 30 January, http://news. nationalgeographic.com/news/2014/01/140130-drug-trafficking-deforestation-central-america-environment-policy-reform/.

34. 'New frontiers or old boundaries?'

35. Teale N. Phelps Bondaroff, Wietse van der Werf and Tuesday Reitano, *The Illegal Fishing and Organized Crime Nexus: Illegal fishing as transnational organised crime* (Geneva: Global Initiative against Transnational Organized Crime, 2015).

36. Kukka Ranta, 'Illicit Migration to Europe: Consequences of Illegal Fishing and Overfishing in West Africa', *Global Initiative against Transnational Organized Crime*, 31 May 2015. http://www.globalinitiative.net/illicit-migration-to-europe-consequences-of-illegal-fishing-and-overfishing-in-west-africa/.

37. Gosling, *The Global Response to Transnational Organised Environmental Crime*.

38. Sarah Chayes, *Thieves of State: Why Corruption Threatens Global Security* (London and New York: W.W. Norton & Company LTD./INC., 2015).

39. 'Organized Crime: A Cross-Cutting Threat to Sustainable Development'.

40. James Cockayne, 'Chasing Shadows: Strategic Responses to Organised Crime in Conflict-Affected Situations', *The RUSI Journal*, vol. 158, no. 2, April 2013, pp. 10–24.

CHAPTER 3

IT and Cyber Capabilities as a Force Multiplier for Transnational Crime

Camino Kavanagh

Abstract The first section of this chapter provides an historical overview of the evolution of criminal use of IT capabilities as a force multiplier, highlighting a number of emblematic cases. The second section assesses more recent uses of IT and cyber capabilities, while the third assesses the strategic and policy implications of transnational crime's use of these capabilities.

Sections one and two are conceived through the lens of a number of 'strategic inflection points' in IT development. These points represent moments when a new development in information technology emerged at the same time as important changes in strategic and geopolitical affairs, allowing states, private enterprise (and later citizens) to extend their interests beyond traditional borders with important implications for traditional notions of sovereignty, questions of strategic reciprocity and international politics. They also facilitated a shift in the scope and scale of criminal activity.

Keywords Cybercrime • Technology • Information • Corruption • Privacy • Citizen security

C. Kavanagh (✉)
Department of War Studies, School of Security Studies,
King's College, London, UK

V. Comolli (ed.), *Organized Crime and Illicit Trade*,
https://doi.org/10.1007/978-3-319-72968-8_3

Transnational crime uses information technology (IT) and cyber capabilities as a force multiplier, enhancing efficiency and effectiveness of operations and reducing overall risk. Criminal use of IT capabilities for these purposes is by no means a new phenomenon. Ever since the invention of the optical telegraph, those with illicit intent have been quick to take advantage of information technology to advance their goals. Over time, and as crime has become more organized and information technologies more sophisticated, IT and cyber capabilities have provided criminal groups with important advantages, particularly as their operations shifted from the purely local to national and global arenas.

Today, states across the globe are struggling to respond to criminal activity enabled by information technologies or conducted within connected systems themselves, that is, the environment commonly referred to in policy circles today as 'cyberspace'. Transnational crime's use of IT and cyber capabilities has diversified significantly. Functions such as communications, surveillance, counter-surveillance, money laundering, logistics and command and control, all enable transnational crime to enhance the efficiency and effectiveness of operations and reduce risk. The links between traditional transnational crime and cybercriminal activity are increasing, and the potential strategic advantages inherent in certain IT and cyber capabilities and services appear to be encouraging a closer relationship between transnational crime and terrorist groups on the one hand, and transnational crime and the state on the other.

Finally, while undoubtedly important, the current focus on cybercrime over-shadows an equally essential discussion of transnational crime's use of IT and cyber capabilities. Certainly, it produces equal, if not more serious, harms to society, yet transnational crime also has important geopolitical, international security and developmental impacts and concomitant implications for human rights, drugs, transnational organized crime and counter-terrorism policies.

The first section of this chapter provides an historical overview of the evolution of criminal use of IT capabilities as a force multiplier, highlighting a number of emblematic cases. The second section assesses more recent uses of IT and cyber capabilities, while the third assesses the strategic and policy implications of transnational crime's use of these capabilities.

Sections one and two are conceived through the lens of a number of 'strategic inflection points' in IT development. These points represent moments when a new development in information technology emerged at the same time as important changes in strategic and geopolitical affairs, allowing states, private enterprise (and later citizens) to extend their interests beyond traditional borders with important implications for traditional notions of sovereignty, questions of strategic reciprocity and international politics. They also facilitated a shift in the scope and scale of criminal activity.

THE PARALLEL EVOLUTION OF INFORMATION TECHNOLOGY AND ORGANIZED CRIME

Early technologies such as the optical and electric telegraphs, radio and telephony provided strategic, operational and tactical value during war, served as geopolitical currency during peace negotiations and led to the emergence of some of the first international regimes aimed at shaping state behaviour in the field of Information Communications Technology (ICT).[1] Later, new developments such as satellite, spy and precision technologies during the Cold War, coupled with second and third generation computers and connected systems emerging from the Defense Advanced Research Projects Agency (DARPA), increased the strategic value of IT capabilities. States openly voiced an increased sense of vulnerability regarding the new technologies, vulnerabilities obviously accentuated by the grammar of the Cold War. The invention of the microchip in the early 1970s brought down the cost of computing enormously, paving the way towards the first personal computers and greater connectivity, as well as enabling greater precision technologies, particularly smart weapons. The privatisation of 'the internet' in the late 1990s, generating heavy reliance on computers and connected systems for government, business, financial and social transactions, brought so many advantages that almost anything—from an Internet service provider (ISP) to a twitter account—can now be designated a strategic asset. The latter has had important societal and geopolitical implications, exacerbated by state's covert uses of the technologies and related capabilities in the name of national and international security. Transnational crime developed alongside these IT-related developments and, like actors in all other sectors, has taken advantage of the technologies to improve the effectiveness of operations and reduce risk.

Crime and Connectivity: The Early Days

The Chappe (or optical) telegraph represents a first strategic inflection point in information technology development in modern history. It shortened the delivery time of messages in unprecedented ways; served a strategic function during the French Revolution and the Napoleonic Wars; and led to the development of the first transnational data network, connecting Denmark and Sweden in 1801 with the objective of serving as an early warning system in the case of attack by Britain.[2] Its founders developed many of the basic principles of today's Internet, including source coding, error detection and signal restoration, control and data signals, inter-operability and routing. The new technology also served as a vector for fraud and new norms of social behaviour.[3]

During this period, crime as we know it today—much less organized crime—was not a principal concern of states. The Chappe telegraph was under French state control from the outset, which used it to relay information from and to the different war fronts, ushering in the first instances of centralised command and control.[4] It was not long, however, before new forms of illicit activity such as financial fraud could be leveraged through the optical cable, with cases in France and the United States representing early examples of high speed trading.[5] For example, in France, a fraud relating to the introduction into regular messages of information about the stock market was discovered in 1836. The case involved two bankers from Bordeaux who had bribed a telegraph operator to modify transmission codes by adding signals to official dispatches, thus allowing them to access information "of the development of the rate of government stocks before the arrival of the press," which was sent by regular post.[6] The fraud and the network of 'pirates and stooges' it employed lasted almost two years. When finally discovered in 1837, the two bankers were tried but acquitted since they had not violated any existing law, that is, the state telegraphic monopoly had not yet been defined by law. Quickly thereafter, and fearing also a proliferation of private networks it would not be able to control, the French government passed a bill banning private networks, the provisions of which remained in place until the twentieth century.[7]

In contrast, in the United States, the optical telegraph was not controlled by the state and speculators soon grasped the advantages of the signalling system for gaining an informational advantage regarding the stock market.[8] While not illegal, the practice became widespread, and set the ball rolling for much more sophisticated forms of fraudulent activity by means of the electric telegraph, the telephone and later the internet, raising important regulatory and legislative challenges for those states that became increasingly dependent on the technologies for government, military and business purposes.

The First Wide-Scale 'Illicit' Use of IT

The emergence of the electric telegraph in 1838 represents a second strategic inflection point in IT development. For the first time in history, an information technology allowed for message storage (enabled by Samuel Morse' code) within the same infrastructure. Two decades later, heads of state marvelled as the first trans-Atlantic message was sent via submarine cable from Valentia island off the West of Ireland to Heart's Content in eastern Newfoundland. In Europe, the revolutionary technology was used to both expand and defend imperial interests far beyond the European Pale, igniting reactions of strategic reciprocity among the major powers who competed to extend their networks across the globe, while maneuvering for access to the resources required to sustain the networks.[9] States—particularly Britain and Germany—exercised enormous authority and control over the technologies. This was equally true in times of peace—through heavy subsidies to the private companies that held the monopoly over the technology—[10] and during war, through legislation that gave them ultimate powers over the technology, its infrastructure and resources (human and financial). In both peace and wartime, states also held ultimate powers over the information flowing through the networks, propelling an equally strategic shift in the field of intelligence.[11] At the same time, unprecedented tensions emerged between the conflicting state interests of "protecting, conserving and controlling information on the one hand, and of importing exporting and exchanging goods [and ideas] on the other—both in pursuit of state goals (in terms of economic expansion) and in support of national policies."[12]

Once again, states were not overly concerned about crime during this period of intense mercantilism. Indeed, the major concern of the time was the sabotage of cables, particularly as cable cutting had become an important tactic in both regular and irregular warfare as well as the focus of heated international discussion prior to and after World War I. Gradually law enforcement agencies began to acknowledge the advantages afforded by the new information technologies for countering crime and as early as the 1840s, used advanced knowledge to apprehend criminal suspects.[13] Yet, it was others that first noticed how the telegraph could be used for illicit gain.

Indeed, the first wide-scale 'illicit' use of information technology can be traced back to the late nineteenth century, when innovations relating to the electric telegraph saw the invention of the ticker—a low-cost and low-maintenance printing telegraph which allowed brokers to monitor transactions on exchange floors. Improved by Western Union employees such as Thomas Edison, the ticker and the quadruplex, a system allowing four messages to be relayed instantly over one telegraph wire, enabled Western Union "to exploit the growing demand for real-time information,"[14] leading to the emergence of organized gambling via so-called 'bucket shops' across the United States. The manner in which bucket shops operated was as risky as it was simple: "quotes from the New York Stock Exchange were piped in, usually illegally, by way of pirated tickers, and the owners of the shops, called 'bucketeers,' acted like the house in a casino, taking bets from the public on whether a stock would rise or fall at any given time."[15]

While many have argued that the scheme helped to democratise speculation in the United States, providing access to those traditionally excluded from high-end exchanges and the accompanying benefits, 'bucketeers' profited enormously as did the telegraph companies,[16] with the companies themselves deriving a significant part of the profit, i.e. "the ostensibly respectable accomplices of the thieves (…) [who] lend eager aid, collecting in exchange for their assistance great slices of the loot of thievery."[17]

Gambling was outlawed in most states at the time, yet, for authorities it was difficult to differentiate between legitimate speculation and illicit gambling hence despite initial attempts by the main exchanges to have them outlawed, the bucket shops flourished and spread across the Union. By the turn of the century the bucket shops had consolidated and were controlled by a syndicate popularly known as 'the Big Four' with their combined transactions reportedly depressing by half and two-thirds the value of a seat on the country's main exchanges, Manhattan and Chicago. The war that ensued between the United States (U.S.) Board of Trade, the telegraph companies and the bucket shops lasted some twenty-five years with the telegraph companies—particularly Western Union—strongly defending the right of the bucketeers to use the information, i.e. stock quotations, provided via the ticker technology as they saw fit. The practice was eventually brought to a close by a Supreme Court ruling that gave stock and commodity exchanges control over their quotations, i.e.

the right to provide or deny its data to whomever they wished,[18] with bucket shop transactions subsequently outlawed in most states.[19] The experience with this early form of rapid communication had an important influence on financial policy and criminal law in the US and embedded in the [Chicago] Board a "growing realisation of its public responsibilities and attempts at self-regulation," helping it establish "a legitimate place in the economic order as an arena for organised speculation by painting bucket shops as evil doers."[20] And while the bucket shops had largely been able to operate due to lack of legislation governing their activities, their emergence signalled the rapidity with which information technology could potentially be adopted for illicit gain; the conflicting role telecommunications providers played in the process; and the challenges legislators and law enforcement officials would face as they strove to keep up.

The Inter-war Years: Law Enforcement Fights Back

During World War I, all powers possessing the capability fully recognised the strategic, operational and tactical surveillance and censorship opportunities offered by telegraph communications, while cutting of enemy cables was accepted by the Allied powers as a legitimate act of warfare.[21] By the end of the war, innovation in the field of wireless radio and telephony had outpaced the electric telegraph, largely curtailing its strategic value. Yet, similar censorship and surveillance possibilities offered by the telegraph and telephony were hardly lost on other non-military services. Nor were they lost on those criminal groups whose operations were threatened by the capabilities.

Indeed, drawing on war-time censorship practices, reliance on wiretapping for criminal investigations became widespread during this period. As soon as the war was over, American criminal investigators turned to telegraph companies for access to records of messages exchanged over the wires. Initially, such investigations related mainly to cases of alleged political corruption with police officers leaning on weak tools such as a subpoena *duces tecum* with limited (if any) judicial oversight to attain access to information when telegraph companies refused to comply. Telegraph companies were later forbidden by law to transmit messages perceived to constitute or further a crime and staff were obliged to send those same messages to law enforcement officials, an obligation that must have been difficult as well as dangerous. Western Union fought hard to maintain its clients' privacy, with courts in cases such as the Missouri Supreme Court's

Ex Parte Brown of 1878 placing a temporary break on unwarranted access to private communications. Organized crime would benefit from these privacy protections as the telephone became the technology of preference for communications.[22]

Already before World War I, privacy concerns had emerged in relation to the spread of telephony, particularly following the public disclosure of what appears to have been the government's first wiretapping programme in which New York Police Department (NYPD) intercepted the calls of Catholic priests suspected of misuse of city funds.[23] Telephone companies' efforts to protect client's Forth amendment rights produced limited results, not least because the period coincided with Prohibition and the emergence of important organized criminal groups, many tied to organized labour. Law enforcement's interest in wiretapping intensified with the famous (or perhaps infamous) Prohibition-era Olmsted v United States case in 1928 which considered Fourth Amendment limitations "on the power of the government to intercept telephone calls."[24] The case involved a number of petitioners convicted for conspiring to violate the National Prohibition Act by unlawfully possessing, transporting and selling alcohol.[25] The evidence to convict the members of the network was obtained through wiretapping conducted over several months, leading to the highly contentious court case involving a curious alignment of telecommunications companies and members of the organized crime racket who argued, unsuccessfully, that the evidence collected through wiretapping constituted a violation of the Fourth Amendment rights. The closely-divided court ruled in favour of the Government although the U.S. Supreme Court later reversed the decision, holding that "the Communications Act of 1934 prohibited wiretapping."[26]

Following on the heels of this case, an important New York City lobby, combining organized labour and organized crime convinced the 1938 Constitutional Convention that wiretapping should be forbidden unless judicially authorised.[27] The lobby to limit government wiretapping grew nationally and aligned itself with the main telecommunications companies bent on protecting client privacy. Wiretapping continued largely unabated until the decision was ultimately overturned in 1967 in Katz v. United States, with the opinion that the Fourth Amendment protects people, not places," and the introduction of the idea of a 'reasonable' expectation of Fourth Amendment protection.[28]

Post-war: The Transformative Years

World War II served as the catalyst for significant advances in IT-related research and development. Encryption technologies, of enormous strategic and tactical value during World War II, were further developed for surveillance and counter-surveillance purposes as telephone and fax became ubiquitous. The computational power of the ENIAC, a computer developed during the war to reduce the [human] computational time required for preparing firing tables, evolved to support the development of nuclear capabilities as well as space-based communications and spy technology, and later radar and precision weapons. The increasing capacity of these technologies to penetrate traditional geographic obstacles, by-passing the state and traditional hard-core defenses, strongly influenced states' approaches to information technology in warfare and international politics.

Once again, these developments did not escape the attention of criminal groups. Crime after the Great War had remained highly localised, with emerging criminal groups in Italy and the United States still linked closely to certain regions (such as the Sicilian mafia which Mussolini had tried unsuccessfully to suppress in the 1920s), neighbourhoods or ports (New York and Chicago's crime gangs). While their criminal enterprise remained largely connected to territory the low barrier access to the new information technologies allowed them to communicate freely and slowly establish footholds nationally and abroad, expand networks and diversify products.

In America, many of the Prohibition-era organized crime groups shifted from alcohol (now legal) to illicit gambling, prostitution and the drug trade, principally cocaine and heroin, and expanded operations across the country. The infamous Appalachian barbecue of 1957 confirmed the existence of national-level syndicates, which only grew in strength over the coming decade.[29] Yet, most efforts and resources remained focused on countering the communist threat, meaning that organized crime continued to flourish and avail of existing and new information technologies to establish and consolidate networks nationally, regionally and globally.

During this period, transnational criminals used IT communications, surveillance and counter-surveillance capabilities as a force multiplier while criminal groups became increasingly wary of using telephones and radio to communicate as law enforcement wiretapping and electronic surveillance efforts began to produce important results. Several cases in the mid- to late-1960s however revealed important unlawful uses of wiretapping and electronic surveillance by Treasury and Justice Department agents in investigations of racketeer influence in Las Vegas casinos, leading to greater scrutiny and restrictions regarding their uses, a development transnational crime evidently benefitted from.[30]

Transnational Crime, IT Capabilities and the Pre-'cyber' Years

The networked computers and enhanced precision technologies emerging in the 1970s represent a forth strategic inflection point in the field of information technology, although the implications of these developments were not fully manifest until the 1990s. Extensive innovation in IT-related research and development (R&D), mainly in the defense and intelligence sectors, led to the emergence of second and third generation computers and the first computer-to-computer networks (ARPANET). Encryption technologies also became more sophisticated. The invention of the microchip in the early 1970s brought down the cost of computing significantly, paving the way towards the first personal computers, greater connectivity and the information revolution. Militaries were quick to harness the new technologies for force multiplication purposes. At the broader societal level, linking information technologies to computers posed important new challenges, for not only could they "remove or transform the locale in which information was kept, but also made [information] accessible from huge distances, and transmittable into different areas or jurisdictions".[31] Moreover, it meant that data and not just code could be manipulated for effect.

The latter decades of the Cold War witnessed the consolidation of existing criminal actors, such as the mafia, and the emergence of new transnational crime groups. For Peter Gastrow, organized crime came of age across the globe in the 1970s and 1980s. As the newly independent states were struggling with the challenges posed by democratisation, broad societal transformation and structural adjustment programmes, a range of transnational criminal groups and networks were "entrench[ing] themselves and develop[ing] significant illicit markets across regions."[32] In the United States, the threats posed by organized crime had become so significant that Congress passed the Racketeer Influenced and Corrupt Organisations (RICO) Act[33] with the objective of "eliminati[ng] the infiltration of organised crime and racketeering into legitimate organisations operating in interstate commerce."[34] The statute was made sufficiently broad to encompass illegal activities relating to any enterprise affecting interstate or foreign commerce, an element that remains highly contested today. At the same time, the reference to 'foreign commerce' confirmed the fact that known criminal groups were extending their reach and establishing contacts and connections, logistical bases and so forth in other regions. And what affected other states, would eventually have domestic implications. These concerns intensified alongside globalisation and the growing inter-dependence of markets.[35] Again, advances in IT (and transport), coupled with new global markets, facilitated the global expansion of illicit activities, freeing criminal organisations from national borders and traditional regional alliances and allowing them to provide or benefit from new services such as forgery and money laundering.

In the United States, the rising trends in organized crime led to the establishment of another Presidential Commission on Organized Crime in 1983[36] which confirmed this diffusion of power away from traditional criminal entities with centralised structures toward non-traditional or networked structures.[37] The report included detailed proposals for amendments regarding existing money-laundering and wiretapping provisions and to the 1978 Right to Financial Privacy Act.[38] It also confirmed the transnational nature of these networks, particularly those involved in illegal narcotics and the intertwining of criminal activity with legitimate business and politics. As U.S. Attorney General of the time warned: "We are in a new period in the government's battle against organized crime, one that requires not just a national but now also an international response."[39] Internationally, limited focus was placed on the transnational dimension of criminal operations and the enabling function of modern technology, due largely to the dual-use nature of the technologies and the fact that questions relating to technology transfer were framed by the more pressing strategic concerns of the Cold War. It would take another 20 years before that international response was realised in the United Nations Convention against Transnational Organized Crime (UNTOC—also known as the Palermo Convention).

The 1970s and 1980s coincided with the first incidences of computer crime, mostly petty phone access theft in the 1970s and increasing hacker incidents in the 1980s, and nothing compared to the huge heists of the 2010s.[40] Undoubtedly, in these first decades of computer crime, illicit activity was highly localised, with the type and frequency of computer crime representing the demographics of the time, notably the number of computers online, the type and amount of online commerce and questions of access and affordability. Provisions on computer and credit card fraud were, however, included in the Comprehensive Crime Control Act of 1984, followed two years later by the Computer Fraud and Abuse Act, and slowly replicated by other, mostly Western states. By the early 1990s, computer-based crime had become significantly more sophisticated, although as with earlier technologies, the principal uses by transnational crime remained financial fraud and money laundering.

The Post-Cold War Years

A fifth strategic inflection point emerged in the 1990s. The gradual spread of connected computers, mobile phones, digital pagers and debit tele-phone cards led to an important growth in numbers of users for both illicit and legitimate purpose.[41] It was however, the privatisation of the 'internet' in the mid-1990s that provoked the most important changes, leading to the advent of e-commerce and growing military and civilian dependency on information technologies.[42] The emergence of the world wide web was a particular driver of this increasing digital dependency, as were other developments such as the laying of the first transatlantic and transpacific fiber optic cables, greater encryption capabilities, wi-fi technology, packet-switching, mobile telephony, social networking services, voice over inter-net protocol, cloud computing and a range of other IT-related products and services. Today, every aspect of modern life (certainly in the developed world) relies on connected computer systems. The different layers consti-tuting this technological sub-strata of modern societies is now said to con-stitute a strategic domain in itself—cyberspace—vulnerable to the effect of malicious use by state and non-state actors alike. At the societal level, criminal activities that earlier represented minor disruptions and petty thievery, now constitute—in all their 'cybered' manifestations—one of the major preoccupations of states, businesses and, increasingly, civil society.

In the post-Cold War years, the information revolution and the focus on globalisation, interdependence and growing inter-connectedness between states and societies suggested that the predictability that had "framed calculative relations between the constitutive units of the interna-tional system" was loosening further, giving rise to important structural changes in the types of relations in which states would have to engage.[43] For example, states would increasingly have to vie for positions, often in competition not just with each other, but also with non-state agencies, whether international corporations, non-governmental organisations, terrorist and extremist groups, and transnational groups and networks trading in illicit goods. Many of these pressures became much more obvious when the boundaries of the Cold War conflict unravelled.

In the United States, groups dominating the underworld for much of the past century were joined by "a chaotic, often violent array of criminal entities, adult gangs and drug-dealing syndicates" operating domestically, regionally and internationally under entirely new and different rules. Longstanding traditional mob moneymakers, including narcotics trafficking, gambling, prostitution, loan-sharking, and labor racketeering, were "augmented by multi-million-dollar financial frauds, money-laundering schemes, identity-theft rackets, and other sophisticated criminal activities that employ the latest electronic and computer gadgetry to subvert legitimate commerce."[44] In Latin America and the Caribbean, groups that had emerged in the 1980s were consolidating their power by the 1990s and, in countries like Colombia, usurping the very authority of the state.

In many instances, organized crime became enmeshed in post-independence conflicts or statebuilding processes.[45] Indeed, the collapse of the Soviet Union and the fog that followed gave organized crime groups access to military hardware as well as highly sophisticated IT capabilities, generally only accessible to states.[46] Russian and Eastern European criminal groups became important service providers to governments and rebel groups in West Africa, embroiled in lengthy and devastating civil wars. In South Africa, the initial post-Apartheid years saw organized crime spread and diversify with greater involvement of transnational crime groups such as China's triads or Nigerian scammers.[47] Meanwhile, drug cartels in South America took advantage of the political and economic chaos in post-conflict transition states to transit their cocaine to Western Europe, more recently through the fragile settings of West Africa.[48] In Colombia, Guatemala, Jamaica and Mexico, criminal networks infiltrated formal political systems, sometimes with their own armed forces, often replacing formal governmental structures by providing security and delivering essential services to citizens heretofore neglected by formal state institutions. Moreover, politically extreme groups, many violent, started to interact more regularly with criminal networks, shifting from one identity to another, from the formal and legitimate to the informal and illicit, further confounding law enforcement. The reach and scope of transnational crime during these decades gradually led to the signing of the aforementioned UNTOC and the emergence of a number of national and regional strategies and legislative actions aimed at responding to its many manifestations.[49]

Transnational crime's use of IT and cyber capabilities for force multiplication purposes have been crucial to these new realities.[50]

LEVERAGING IT AND CYBER CAPABILITIES

Surveillance and Counter-Surveillance

By the time the Soviet Union collapsed in the late 1980s, many existing criminal groups had already acquired significant IT capabilities and had significant resources at their disposal to meet or outpace those of the most advanced states. The strategic and political void left in those early post-Cold War years, coupled with the freer movement of goods and people enabled by greater interdependence and connectivity, meant that organized criminal groups could spread risk and operate at an even greater scale. Narcotics trafficking in Latin America and the Caribbean reached its zenith, with extremely violent groups morphing from somewhat localised entities to ones with global reach. Increasingly sophisticated IT could also be leveraged to defend the organisation's assets and interests against potential threats. The new technologies included cellular phones and digital pagers,[51] while surveillance circumvention tactics and tools included the use of debit telephone cards, phone switching and increasingly sophisticated computing and encryption technologies.

An early manifestation of this new reality was already evident in 1994 in a case involving the Cali drug cartel. By the mid-1990s, the cartel was responsible for approximately 80% of the global cocaine supply, with an annual turnover of US$7 billion. Within the organisation, Santacruz Londoño was responsible for the cartel's intelligence collection effort.[52] In 1994, police accidentally discovered a computer centre manned in shifts around the clock by four to six technicians in a building owned by a Cali cartel front man working directly with Londoño. The facility boasted a US$1.5 million IBM AS400 mainframe, the kind once used by banks. The super computer was networked with half a dozen terminals and monitors and reportedly held a database of residential and office phone numbers of U.S. diplomats and agents (both known and suspected American law enforcement, intelligence, and military operatives) based in Colombia. In addition, the phone company (which had been infiltrated by the organized crime group) was supplying the cartel with complete records of all telephone calls in the form of the originating and destination phone numbers. The cartel had used custom-designed software to cross-reference the phone company records against their own list of suspected law enforcement, military, and intelligence officials or agents to produce a list of potential informants.[53] The extensive wealth at the disposal of the Cali cartel and similar organisations allowed them to purchase "the latest and most sophisticated state-of-the art" IT equipment, which was used to control every phase of business, and everyone operating as part of it.[54] The latter created significant headaches for law enforcement agencies who were unable to keep up technologically.[55] Other groups, for example some of the Mexican drug cartels, would later establish IT companies to provide services to their own networks, while IT companies such as Sitel in Calabria, Italy, maintained dubious links with members of mafia networks.[56]

The realisation of the power inherent in these and other IT capabilities led to a flurry of government responses in the United States. For example, in 1994, the U.S. Congress adopted the Communications Assistance for Law Enforcement Act (CALEA) requiring "wireline and wireless carriers to meet written standards of technical compliance to ensure rapid response to court orders for lawful intercepts."[57] Subsequently in 1995, the U.S. President invoked the International Emergency Economic Powers Act (IEEPA),[58] declaring a national emergency (via Executive Order),[59] to deal with the threat posed by significant foreign narcotics traffickers in Colombia and the harm they caused in the United States.[60] Soon after, the government adopted the Specially Designated Narcotics Traffickers (SDN) list—around which the 1999 Foreign Narcotics Kingpin Designation Act, would be shaped. The SDN list included some 527 companies and some 815 individuals involved in ownership or management of the 21 Colombian drug cartel leaders' business empires, including radio and communications companies. In 2006, the updated SDN list included IT companies and services enabling narcotics trafficking.[61] Yet, these mechanisms failed to address cases involving dual-use technologies and experts providing technical services to transnational crime.

For instance, more than a decade later, the Zetas, a Mexican drug cartel, was discovered to have established an extensive shadow communications network to "conduct encrypted conversations" outside the official cell phone network.[62] The radio network, established with legally available material, stretched from the Texas border through the Gulf region and down into Guatemala. The person responsible for establishing the network was Jose Luis del Toro Estrada—also known as *El Técnico*—arrested by the Drug Enforcement Administration (DEA) in 2008 in Houston, Texas, and later sentenced for conspiracy to distribute cocaine. According to his plea agreement, del Toro acknowledged that he had been responsible for establishing the system in most of Mexico's 31 states and parts of northern Guatemala "under the orders of the top leaders in the Gulf cartel and the Zetas."[63] Cartel bosses in each drug-smuggling territory were "responsible for buying towers and repeaters as well as equipping underlings with radios and computers." Del Toro was also responsible for "employing specialists to run the network and research new technology."[64] This elaborate system also allowed the highest-ranking Zeta operatives to engage in highly encrypted communications over the Internet. Joint U.S.-Mexican investigations have since led to several arrests and the seizure of some 167 antennas, 155 repeaters, 166 power sources, 71 pieces of computer equipment, and 1,446 radios.[65] Other cartels operating in Mexico are reported to have also developed similar, albeit narrower in territorial scope, IT and communications systems. The dual-use nature of the technology used in these instances evidently limits the possibility of sales restrictions or sanctions while the availability of capabilities required to conduct effective surveillance or counter-surveillance are readily available and easily accessible from lawful malware providers (such as FinFisher).

Corruption

Corruption is a major enabling factor in organized criminal activity, not only to move goods but also to access the technologies required to circumvent law enforcement and surveil potential enemies and witnesses. Cases from over a decade demonstrate the ease with which organized crime can access high-grade IT hardware, normally restricted to states, and take advantage of official corruption.

Shaheed Roger Khan was probably the most well-known career criminal in Guyana until his arrest by American officials in 2006. Khan ran a paramilitary troop known as 'The Phantom Squad' which ruthlessly terrorised and eliminated those who threatened to undermine his activities. Between 2002 and 2006 some 200 people are said to have been murdered by the Phantom Squad.[66] Before his eventual arrest in Suriname and subsequent extradition from Trinidad to the U.S., Khan enjoyed relatively free reign in Guyana, either operating directly with the government or with its tacit acquiescence. Khan was a major exporter of Colombian cocaine to the United States, the United Kingdom and Canada. He traded cocaine for arms, often acting as a middleman in such exchanges between Colombia (particularly the Fuerzas Armadas Revolucioarias de Colombia, FARC), Suriname, and French Guyana.

In 2002, Khan was arrested with two others—one a member of the Guyana Police Force—for possession of a cache of weapons and IT equipment—including computers, cellular intercept equipment and other electronic devices with digitised electronic maps and plans of the capital, Georgetown and certain East Coast villages.[67] While a magistrate's court later dismissed the charges against the three, the electronic intelligence devices, including high-grade cellular intercept equipment (a CSM 7806 surveillance device), found in Khan's possession were traced back to a United Kingdom (UK)-based firm (Smith Myers), which maintained it had sold it to the government of Guyana. In fact, Guyana's Minister of Health gave Khan permission to purchase the equipment on behalf of the government via the company's Florida sales office. A representative of Smith Myers Communications then traveled to Guyana to train Khan in its use. While further evidence has since emerged connecting both Khan and the Minister of Health to the case,[68] the government has consistently resisted calls to investigate; the Speaker of Parliament disallowed a motion to investigate the link between the Minister of Health and Khan.[69] Cases like this abound, with links between government, organized crime and business undermining effective responses to transnational crime or compliance with mechanisms such as sanctions lists or export controls.[70]

The latter is all the more relevant as states begin to include information technologies in sanctions within the framework of broader geopolitical conflict and tensions.[71] The latter runs the risk of creating a black market for the technologies, pushing their uses further into the so-called 'dark web,' or unwittingly providing the state against which the sanction are provided with a (much-undesired) monopoly over the telecommunications or IT market.[72]

Logistics

Transnational crime uses the latest technologies for global operational support, with armies of fixers and enablers fulfilling the logistical roles required to ensure the movement of goods. In the early 2010s, computer hackers were formally identified as core enablers of the global illicit trade. Described by the European Police Office (EUROPOL) as a "professional, continuously evolving, service-based criminal industry driv[ing] the innovation of tools and methods used by criminals and facilitat[ing] the digital underground through a multitude of complementary services," this new form of fixer or enabler can also "extend attack capacity to those otherwise lacking the skills or capabilities."[73]

Traditional organized crime groups have used the new "service-based nature of the cybercrime market"[74] to carry out more sophisticated crimes, buying access to the technical skills required to move illicit goods. Merging traditional modes of operation with those available for hire online, an organized crime group involving Belgian, Dutch, Turkish and Peruvian nationals was apprehended in June 2013 for attempting to smuggle cocaine and heroin through the Belgian port of Antwerp.[75] Using hacker services, the criminal group managed to take control of the computers running two container terminals and a harbor company. The drug trafficking group, operating out of the Netherlands and Belgium, is believed to have been using this *modus operandi* for over a two-year period from June 2011, using Belgian hackers to infiltrate computer networks in at least two companies operating in the port of Antwerp to ensure safe passage of heroin and cocaine hidden among legitimate cargo. According to the case file, the hackers were internationally known computer experts ('white hackers') who had often been consulted by Belgian and foreign authorities on security issues. This was apparently the first time they were caught engaged in criminal activities.[76]

The computer breaches allowed hackers to virtually infiltrate the legal infrastructure of the companies, from where they could "access secure data giving them the location and security details of containers," which in turn allowed traffickers to collect the illicit cargo before the legitimate owner arrived.[77] They used classic intrusion methods such as emails with attachments containing Trojans sent to employees. When the initial breach was discovered, hackers then broke into the companies' offices to install logging devices (keyloggers and penetration testing tools) to capture passwords. The existence of these devices was eventually discovered after ICT employees detected network problems.[78]

According to the case officers, this was the first time such a *modus operandi* was discovered by law enforcement. The incident was also linked to an incident in Limburg province in which a truck driver who had unintentionally driven off with a cargo of cocaine was shot at by assailants using AK-47 assault rifles. The dismantling of the operation eventually led to a series of raids by Dutch and Belgian police and the arrest of 15 suspects on charges of criminal organisation, hacking and drug trafficking. The suspects—since been released on parole—face sentences of up to ten years.[79]

Already, huge ports such as the one in Antwerp faced significant challenges in dealing with traditional breaches by organized crime. Reports such as the Brookings Institution study "The Critical Infrastructure Gap: U.S. Port Facilities and Cyber Vulnerabilities," while focused on more strategic vulnerabilities and threats, highlights the degree to which even the most developed states have not afforded attention to cybersecurity risks to port facilities.

The hybrid nature of the incident at Antwerp Port suggests significant challenges ahead, particularly in those settings where law enforcement has limited capacity to deal with these kind of hybrid challenges. Indeed, United Nations Office on Drugs and Crime (UNODC) experts suggest that while port authorities across Europe and other regions are now familiar with this case, developing sustainable mechanisms to respond to these emerging challenges will be difficult, not least because of the capacity requirements across sectors. In this specific case:

> the Belgian police [was] not well-prepared for handling cases like this. We don't have the knowledge, the means and experience to conduct investigations in cases in which a criminal drug organisation relies on experienced hackers to serve their goal. We were lucky that the "white" hackers did not have experience in keeping under the police-radars in the real world. In their virtual, digital habitat they did not make mistakes, we caught them because of their actions in real life (use of cellular phones during burglaries).[80]

Certainly, as noted by the head of EUROPOL, the growing trend in adopting "the cybercrime features of a more transient, transactional and less structured organizational model" may reflect how all serious crime will be organized in the future, presenting advantages to criminal groups and others operating on land and on the sea and posing serious challenges to law enforcement.[81]

Fomenting Fear

Fomenting fear has long been a tactic of terrorist groups with groups such as al-Qaeda and the so-called Islamic State (ISIS) using modern information technology, particularly social platforms on the internet, to that end. Transnational criminal groups now appear to be using similar methods to monitor negative on-line coverage of their activities and foment terror among the population.[82] This can be dangerous especially in areas where the traditional media has already been silenced by criminal groups, government agencies or business elites. In such instances, citizens take up policing functions themselves, using blogging sites or social platforms such as Twitter to fill the void left by weak and corrupt police forces or a silenced or co-opted traditional media. Mexico is a case in point. Here main media outlets have largely ceased covering 'drug-war stories' and have been largely replaced by bloggers, who now face enormous risks.[83]

In late 2011, several bloggers working out of Nuevo Laredo, Mexico, were killed by members of drug cartels who berated them *post-facto* for participating in online discussions about drug trafficking in the country and tipping off authorities about their activities. Victims were beheaded or disemboweled, and messages such as "this happened to me because I didn't understand I shouldn't post things on social networks" were inscribed on what was left of their bodies.[84] In October 2014, another blogger using the handle "Miut3" was kidnapped and killed in Reynosa, Tamaulipas. Using her blog and Twitter account (with over 41,000 followers), Maria del Rosario regularly sent out information on situations of risk as well as updates on drug trafficking incidents. In this specific case, the drug cartel took over her social media page, posting warnings about her imminent death, as well as photos of her body after being kidnapped and killed.[85] Mexican bloggers and journalists fear that the recent attacks will prevent people from using the internet and social platforms to circulate information on what is happening in different parts of the country. Indeed, a 2013 survey of some 102 journalists and bloggers across 20 Mexican states revealed that "nearly 70% [had] been threatened or [have] suffered attacks because of their work." In addition, 96% said "they know of colleagues who have been attacked.[86] Survey respondents also noted cyber-espionage and email account cracking by both criminal organisations and governmental agencies as "the most serious digital risks they face."[87]

Meanwhile, in light of the attacks on bloggers, the hacktivist group Anonymous established 'OpCartel,' an operation that threatened to release details of Zeta operatives and collaborators obtained through hacking into the emails of Mexican government officials.[88] Following the alleged kidnapping of an Anonymous member by the Zetas, and the threat to kill ten individuals for each collaborator identified, Anonymous publicly abandoned its OpCartel campaign.[89] In 2010, two Mexican students at

Columbia University in New York City tracking information on organized crime-related violence in Monterrey were also stopped in their tracks. The U.S.-based site administrator received threatening phone calls, after which the project was cancelled.[90]

This inability to capture citizen information and empirical data seriously undermines attempts to build effective responses to violence, organized crime and drug trafficking. Important efforts have been made, for example by the Igarrape Institute in Brazil, to map efforts to reduce violence using ICTs.[91] This approach relies on those at risk safely accessing the internet, social networks, mobile phones and blogging platforms and circumventing surveillance. Yet, while bloggers and journalists largely rely on the Internet, social networks, mobile phones and blogging platforms for their work, they have little or no command of digital security tools such as encryption, use of virtual private networks (VPNs), anonymous Internet navigation and secure file removal. Providing at-risk citizens with these tools has become a priority for some actors, including tech companies, software developers, non-governmental organisations (NGOs), human rights organisations and some government agencies.

Services Providers

At the same time, the widespread availability of these digital security tools has been an important enabler of transnational criminal activity, including child pornography, trading in illicit goods, money laundering, and even forced labour. A six-month probe into the anonymity tool Tor suggested that some 80 hidden services relate to paedophilia,[92] leading U.S. Assistant Attorney General, Leslie Caldwell to decry the companies developing the technology.[93]

The small-scale (in volume) yet significant number of people involved in peddling illicit goods online has surged in recent years, enabled by the 'Dark Web' and made infamous by SilkRoad, an international platform allegedly managed by Ross Ulbricht (aka Dread Pirate, DPR, Silk Road) and characterised as "the most sophisticated and extensive criminal marketplace on the Internet".[94] According to the official indictment, the SilkRoad website was used by "several thousand drug dealers and other unlawful vendors to distribute hundreds of kilos of illegal drugs and other illicit goods and services[95] to well over a hundred thousand buyers worldwide, and to launder hundreds of millions of dollars deriving from these unlawful transactions".[96] Ulbricht was arrested in October 2013. Some expected him to be charged under the RICO statute, which as noted by WIRED's Kevin Poulsen, "has given the U.S. a powerful new legal weapon as it takes on a growing number of underground criminal forums dealing in everything from weapons to drugs to more cybercrime."[97] For example, David Ray Camez, a 22-year old American citizen was charged and sentenced for internet fraud and later convicted for racketeering and conspiracy to commit racketeering under the RICO statute. This meant that a low-level criminal was held "legally culpable for every crime committed by all 7,900 users of Carder.su, the identify theft forum where he bought stolen credit card information and counterfeiting equipment for use in his crimes" and could be sentenced to 20 years in prison.[98]

Ulbricht's fate looks no better. He was brought to trial on seven charges including drug trafficking, conspiracy to commit money laundering, conspiracy to commit computer hacking, murder-for-hire and a so-called kingpin charge. Ulbricht was ultimately found guilty on all seven counts and now faces a minimum of 30 years in prison. As for Silk Road, the site was taken down; eight others were arrested for selling drugs. According to court documents, the website had facilitated US$1.2 billion worth of transactions and collected US$80 million in commission fees in less than three years.

Nonetheless, it is not clear that the investigation and prosecution were worth the cost and effort since the Silk Road community is still thriving. Just five weeks after Silk Road was shut down, another site with the same name emerged, Silk Road 2.0, with an oddly democratic ethos:

> As everyone is now aware, the previous Silk Road has fallen. For law enforcement worldwide this was a small victory for them where they would receive a pat on the back from their superiors and maybe a good Christmas bonus (…). However, what law enforcement has failed to understand is the consequences of their actions. Silk Road is not one man. Silk Road is an idea, and where Silk Road now lies is in the people who made it what it was and it is those people who will, with a little help, bring the idea back to life again under a new name.[99]

Silk Road 2.0 has since been brought down. Yet, beyond the two Silk Roads, there is an expanding "horde of existing marketplaces and upstarts, all looking to become the next online drug empire."[100] These include BlackMarket Reloaded (BMR), Sheep Marketplace, Project:Black Flag, Deepbay, Drug Market, Brain Market, Budster and more recently Evolution, all vying for customers and some like BMR even posting details about volume of trade.[101] Some have been taken down through highly effective law enforcement efforts such as Operation Onymous, yet these 'dark web' sites keep popping up, engaging law enforcement in a constant game of whack-a-mole.[102]

Ensuring the means (legislative, technological, financial and other) to fight the 'dark web' and increasingly sophisticated encryption technologies has, in consequence, become a priority of government agencies across the globe, accentuating existing tensions between citizens and the state, notably around issues of privacy. In the United States, law enforcement agencies describe these activities as 'going dark' in the sense that those responsible for protecting citizens are not always in a position "to access the evidence need[ed] to prosecute crime and prevent terrorism even with lawful authority."[103] In the words of the Director of the Federal Bureau of Investigation (FBI): "we have the legal authority to intercept and access communications and information pursuant to court order, but we often lack the technical ability to do so." Again, tensions between technology, law enforcement, citizen rights and public safety move to the fore.

Command and Control

In 2008, ten men with access to the internet and armed with weapons and across-the-counter IT and cyber capabilities brought Mumbai, a city of some 20 million inhabitants, to a complete standstill, killing some 172 people and injuring more than 300. As in the case of Colombian and Mexican drug cartels, the Mumbai terrorists developed a sophisticated, yet low-cost platform to guide their operations. They carried mobile and satellite phones, had access to satellite imagery and used night vision goggles. More importantly, backup support was provided by an operations centre located across the border in Pakistan. The operations centre conducted real-time monitoring of traditional and social media coverage of the massacre, identified hotel guests, and issued orders to kill.[104] The innovative use of the operations centre gave the terrorists unprecedented situational awareness and tactical advantages over the police and government officials, and they used these advantages to great effect.

Organized criminal groups have access to many of these same capabilities, even if they might use them for less violent and non-ideological purposes. For example, in December 2014, some 76 Chinese nationals were accidentally discovered manning a cybercrime command and control cell around the clock in an upscale district of Nairobi, Kenya. According to the Chinese Embassy in Nairobi, the groups' capabilities were basic (largely identity theft) while the targets of the groups' cybercrime activities were Chinese nationals in China.[105] The Kenyan government, however, alleged that the capabilities at the disposal of the cell "could have disrupted Kenya's communication systems and infiltrated bank accounts and money transfer networks."[106] The detainees are facing initial charges of cross-border telecommunication fraud and electronically swindling over 100m yuan (US$16.5m) from Chinese victims.

A diplomatic spat ensued between the two governments, with China insisting that the suspects be extradited for further investigation and prosecution in China because the victims are in China, while Kenya is dragging its feet, insisting on due process, and further investigation, before reaching a decision on extradition. Indeed, other more strategic concerns have been raised, leading Kenya's Director of Criminal Investigations to "rope in experts to tell us if the [accused] were committing crimes of espionage (…) These people seem to have been brought here specifically for a mission which we are investigating."[107] Nonetheless, law enforcement officials from both countries eventually cooperated in the investigation and the suspects were eventually deported to China. What was not revealed until later was that the individuals were actually Taiwanese, not Chinese. This situation led to further tensions, this time between Taiwanese and Kenyan officials, the former concerned about the fate of its citizens once back on Chinese soil. In 2017, a similar situation surfaced in Spain concerning some 200 Taiwanese nationals involved in a massive telecom fraud staged from Spain and targeting individuals in mainland China.[108] Both cases highlighted not just the innovative nature of these kinds of crimes in terms of scope and geographic location of victim and perpetrator, but also a number of jurisdictional, diplomatic, geopolitical and potential human rights issues not usually factored into traditional responses to transnational crime.

While the outcome is still pending, the case demonstrates how a large group of foreign nationals in a sophisticated transnational criminal network managed to pass unnoticed in one of Africa's key urban centers. Such remote command and control cells could someday be used by other actors, including states, and for much more malevolent purposes.

STRATEGIC IMPLICATIONS AND POLICY PERSPECTIVES

Transnational crime is not going away anytime soon; rather, if anything, it appears to be thriving, enabled in large part by information technologies. Indeed, the failure to respond to transnational crime and these new challenges can have a serious impact on national governance structures and ultimately regional and international security, as captured in a number of Security Council Presidential Statements over the past years and the United Nations Secretary General's December 2014 synthesis report.[109] The World Economic Forum (WEF) suggests that "criminal networks have expanded into multi-billion dollar syndicates, harnessing the illicit trade of people, goods, drugs, money, intellectual property and environmental resources" with "estimates of the shadow economy plac[ing] the scale of the issue at US\$ 650bn, or a staggering US\$ 2 trillion including money laundering." For the first time, for example, transnational crime has been placed on the development agenda and its eradication is now included among the Sustainable Development Goals (Goal 16) as discussed in Chap. 2.[110] Importantly, the 2015 Global Risk Report identified the failure of national governance—provoked, *inter alia,* by transnational crime and illicit trade—as the third most likely geopolitical risk, following interstate conflict and state collapse or crisis.[111] Other related risks included technological ones such as cyber attacks, data fraud or theft, misuse of technologies and the risk of critical infrastructure breakdown.[112]

These geopolitical, developmental and technological realities and risks are important to bear in mind when responding to transnational crime and its growing use of IT and cyber capabilities, not least because of their implications for a range of issue and policy areas.

Human Rights

Throughout history, it has never taken criminal organisations long to determine how to take advantage of new technologies. IT has been a particular enabler of criminal activity and law enforcement and legislators have consistently tried to keep apace. Yet, this has often meant developing tools and mechanisms to monitor criminal actors, which if abused—as has often been the case—create enormous friction between privacy rights and national security prerogatives. The perception of abuse of these capacities and capabilities has been exacerbated in recent times by instruments such as the 2001 U.S. Patriot Act, with important repercussions elsewhere.[113]

The 2013 Snowden revelations on U.S. and UK monitoring and surveillance practices only served to exacerbate existing tensions. There is a growing perception that such practices have undermined the basis upon which norms of responsible state behavior can be shaped, with other states—democratic or otherwise—emulating such intrusive behaviour in the name of national security, posing important risks to citizens around the globe.

In addition, IT and telecommunications companies (and more recently ISPs) have found themselves at the centre of this friction between privacy rights and national security prerogatives (or rather client's interests and the state's). On the one hand, some companies are playing an important role in shaping norms of state behavior and safe-guarding client's interests against government intrusion; on the other, they are involved in developing the very tools and technologies adopted by criminal actors or acquiesced to government requests to develop IT/cyber tools and capabilities for addressing growing 'going dark' concerns. Some voices in the United States are arguing for greater regulatory authority in light of existing and emerging Tor and strong encryption capabilities, suggesting that current lawful intercept capabilities have gone "from dark to pitch black."[114] CALEA was updated by the Federal Communications Commission (FCC) in 2006, extending its reach to "the internet, broadband or over-the-top providers whose services transited the public switched telephone network." While the legislation has still fallen behind new technologies, intrusive surveillance techniques—such as lawful malware—have been used since at least 1999[115] and do not necessarily require a court order or cooperation with a telecoms provider.[116] Hence, rather than new laws, some suggest that law enforcement actors already "have an abundance of technologies to draw on that go far beyond what CALEA supports or allows," and "can draw on other laws to ensure the legitimacy of their action." Yet, such an approach ventures into the dangerous territory of 'technological solutionism' and will likely increase mistrust between citizen, state and private enterprise.[117] In this regard, the recommendations of a report by the British Intelligence and Security Parliamentary Committee, established after the first Snowden revelations in 2013, might bear more weight: clearer legislation outlining what security agencies can and cannot do, effective oversight mechanisms, and improving public understanding of—and retaining confidence in—the work of the intelligence and security agencies."[118] The latter was spelled out in more detail in a report by a group focused on internet governance:

The obligation of states to protect and promote rights to privacy and free-dom of expression are not optional. (...) Even if they are not absolute rights, limitations to these rights, even those based on national security con-cerns, must be prescribed by law, guaranteeing that exceptions are both necessary and proportionate. Governments should guarantee the same human rights protection to all individuals within their borders.[119]

Global Drug Policy

Most cases discussed in this chapter involve narcotics trafficking. Any drug law enforcement agency would admit that drug cartels—both new and old—outmatch (and will continue outmatching) state cyber/IT law enforcement resources. The cartels have significant funds to spend on acquiring the latest technologies and recruiting tech experts to run and maintain their systems (with many unaware they are working for an illicit enterprise) so as to ensure their products reach their destination.

Law enforcement has undoubtedly made huge progress in responding to the drug trade, yet, as in the past, it will continue to play catch-up, particu-larly as information technology becomes more sophisticated and encryption technologies more difficult to break. Legislating against future crimes has never been an option, even if one can forecast the type of criminal activity likely to emerge around IT innovation.[120] And recent practice has demon-strated that unfettered monitoring and surveillance practices, or bullying tech companies into providing backdoors to anonymity tools, does not work well in democracies where privacy concerns still matter. This means that the cost of interdiction efforts will continue to increase, placing huge burdens on societies across the globe. It is, therefore, perhaps time to refocus global drug policy to deal with those elements of the drug trade that create most harm to society, shifting to a public health-driven policy rather than one almost entirely centred on interdiction, as is currently the case. Current preparations for the 2016 UNGASS on global drug policy will be a starting point, but these crime-IT-related issues are completely absent from current debates, largely over-shadowed by the current focus on cyber-crime and its impact on gross domestic product (GDP) and the global economy.

Global Policy on Transnational Organized Crime

As noted in the previous section, after years of deliberation, UNTOC was adopted in Palermo, Italy in 2000. Some 15 years later, it is clear that the overall impact of the Palermo Convention has been limited. The growing use of information technologies and cyber capabilities by transnational crime is placing additional pressure on an already outdated law enforcement response. A much more informed public debate on both the Palermo Convention (impact and implementation challenges) and the obstacles to reaching agreement on the nature of a cybercrime convention is thus warranted. More effort should also be placed on assessing existing mechanisms such as mutual legal assistance treaties (MLATs),[121] sanctions and trade restrictions, and deepening discussion and sharing lessons on how to respond to transnational crime's use of dual-use technology and its increasing reliance on hackers as enablers of illicit flows.

More citizen-driven approaches to combatting crime have certainly emerged over the past years, particularly in developing countries and driven in large part by the violence associated with transnational crime. Yet, the growing use of IT and cyber capabilities by criminal actors and groups means that concepts such as predictive policing and other technologically-driven solutions aimed at modelling human virtue are gaining traction, removing emphasis once again from the very structural societal issues underlying criminal activity. Hence, as with global drug policy, an important debate on the nature of policing and combating crime is well overdue. It should involve a serious rethink of current U.S.-driven criminological approaches relying on situational crime prevention rather than earlier strategies centred on the underlying social conditions that actually drive crime.[122]

Countering Terror and Transnational Crime: Getting the Twain to Meet

The links between terror and transnational crime have always been difficult to establish, not least because of the dynamic nature of actors and the ease with which they shift between legitimate and illicit activity. According to a study by West Point's 'Countering Terrorism' research team, terrorists and transnational criminals form part of the same global network rather than separate networks. Within this global network, these actors converge around financial, rather than political or ideological interests.[123] In terms of IT and cyber capabilities, this convergence is most likely in developed settings (not in failed or weak states), with transnational crime providing important IT services and products to terrorist groups, including hacking, access to zero-day vulnerabilities, money-laundering, carding (for financing), forged identities and documentation, access to high-grade monitoring and surveillance equipment, and technological advice and expertise.

In this regard, it will be important to develop a deeper understanding of the links between transnational crime's and terrorism's uses of IT and cyber capabilities, how and when these converge and how to more effectively respond.

International Security

As noted in the WEF 2015 Global Risk Report, there are growing concerns that inter-state conflict might again become a common feature of international relations, rather than a tragic feature of our past. Among the broad range of issues associated with these concerns is how information technologies and cyberspace are being used by states for foreign policy purposes against both foes and allies.

For example, there is increasing evidence that states are using criminal groups as proxies to advance foreign policy aims. States' use of proxies is certainly not a new phenomenon. Indeed, states have historically used rebel groups, militias, terrorist and criminal groups to advance their interests. Today the concern is rooted in the high probability that some states are using criminal groups as proxies to conduct malicious cyber attacks against other states, thus allowing them plausible deniability. In response, a number of states are pushing for agreement on a norm "whereby states agree not to conduct or knowingly support online activity that intentionally damages infrastructure or impairs the use of critical infrastructure that provides services to the public."[124] Perhaps this might work, although given the pervasive lack of trust of, and between governments surrounding cyberspace and ICTs, an agreement on the use of proxies is unlikely, the 'proxy for hire' business is likely to thrive, and transnational crime is sure to seek a stake in the business, not least because it can easily acquire the capabilities and resources required to engage in such activity.[125] Building trust between states is thus imperative.

At the national and regional level, information technologies are enabling a growing number of external actors (state and non-state, legitimate and illicit) to become enmeshed in intra-state conflicts, all with different aims and objectives. In many instances (Syria, Iraq, Ukraine), belligerents are increasingly using IT capabilities for a range of purposes, the stronger adversary generally controlling domestic resources and capabilities. Some external actors provide IT-related support to the weaker parties to the conflict; others can sell it to the highest bidder. Yet others punish those (largely state actors or elites with ties to the government) linked to IT products or services that violate human rights via sanctions. As noted, the latter runs the risk of creating a black market for the technologies, pushing their trade and their uses further into the so-called 'dark web,' or unwittingly providing the state against which the sanctions are targeted with a monopoly over the telecommunications or IT market.

In this regard, developing crime-sensitive tools to assess the near-term impacts and longer-term risks of legitimate IT support or sanctions is also imperative.

Geopolitical Considerations

Over the past few years, there have been growing concerns of how urban centers and sprawling megacities, particularly those sitting along the littorals of Eurasia, Africa, and Latin America, will become the centre of gravity for future warfare.[126] Already, many of these agglomerations, home to an inexhaustible source of tech-savvy yet unemployed youth, are highly dynamic centers of online and offline national and transnational criminal activity. There is also an important risk that many of these countries which boast an important technological skill base, a good enough cyberspace infrastructure but weak national governance structures and norms, will be used by transnational criminals to further their geographic reach and broaden their illicit business portfolio.[127] It is likely that much of the IT and cyber infrastructures in many of the existing and emerging megacities will fall outside the scope of formal governance structures, posing even greater advantages to transnational crime, and even greater headaches to law enforcement. Sheldon surmises that the IT and cyber infrastructures in such settings will most likely be "a hybrid mix comprising hardware from commercial carriers on one hand and improvised, often illegally acquired, hardware and networks jury-rigged by technically competent individuals in particular neighborhoods and communities" within megacities such as Mumbai, Karachi, Accra and Nairobi. A number of cases demonstrate how many of the young, tech-savvy unemployed youth in these cities are hired by more seasoned transnational crime groups for identity theft, carding, online gold harvesting, money laundering and forced micro-labour. The very cyber infrastructure of these cities, coupled with structural challenges such as endemic corruption and weak law enforcement capacity, will make it ever more difficult for law enforcement to detect these forms of illicit activity. And should inter- or intra-state conflict break out, the possibilities of recruitment are enormous. It is certainly an issue worth considering in global policy, particularly considering the inter-linkages of transnational crime, development, international security and information technology and cyberspace.

Finally, and in closing, suffice to say that transnational crime has been a very effective user of IT and cyber capabilities for force multiplication purposes. From the early days, even before crime became veritably trans-national, IT capabilities and resources have allowed those with illicit intent to achieve their aims. Legislators and law enforcement have consistently struggled to keep apace, yet solutions have generally been found, often provoking tensions between security and citizen rights, to which solutions have also been found, albeit often imperfect ones. Conversely, as we slip into what many have labelled 'The Internet of Things' and a realisation of how the latter will most likely further enable transnational crime, it will be important to ensure that the same technologies that are part of the problem are not the sole driver of solutions. Instead, such solutions should be informed by public debate, and a much deeper understanding of the *societal* factors *driving* transnational criminal activity instead of simply focusing on the *technological* factors *enabling* it.

NOTES

1. Camino Kavanagh, forthcoming.
2. Gerard J. Holzmann, and Björn Pehrson, *The Early History of Data Networks* (Los Alamitos, CA: IEEE Computer Society Press, 1994).
3. J.M. Dilhac, *The Telegraph of Claude Chappe: An Optical Telecommunication Network for the XVIIIth Century*, http://www.ieeeghn.org/wiki/images/1/17/Dilhac.pdf [No date of publication available, accessed on 14/12/2015].
4. The first message relayed on 15 August 1794 was a military communique reporting French success in retaking the city of Le Quesnoy from the Austrians and the Prussians.
5. Bob Pisani, 'Plundered by Harpies: Early Examples of High-Speed Trading', *Financial History*, issue 111, fall 2014, www.MoAF.org.
6. Patrice Flichy, 'The Birth of Long Distance Communication. Semaphore Telegraphs in Europe (1790–1840)', *Réseaux*, vol. 1, no.1, 1993, pp. 81–101.
7. The exploitation of information technology for control purposes has strong resonances with contemporary experiences in many states (Dilhac, 2009). For a detailed discussion on this case, see C. Kavanagh,

"Information Technology and the State: The Long View". Doctoral thesis. King's College London.

8. Pisani, 'Plundered by Harpies: Early Examples of High-Speed Trading'.

9. Johnathan Reed Winkler, *Nexus: Strategic Communications and American Security in World War I* (Cambridge MA: Harvard University Press, 2008)

10. Ibid.; Daniel R. Headrick, *The Invisible Weapon: Telecommunications and International Politics 1851–1945* (New York: Oxford University Press 1991), Kavanagh, forthcoming.

11. John Keegan, *Intelligence in War*, (London: Vintage, 2004 ed.); Winkler, *Nexus: Strategic Communications and American Security in World War I*; Headrick, *The Invisible Weapon: Telecommunications and International Politics 1851–1945*.

12. Allan Gottlieb, Charles Dalfen and Kenneth Katz, 'The Transborder Transfer of Information by Communications and Computer Systems: Issues and Approaches to Guiding Principles', *The American Journal of International Law*, vol. 68, issue 2, April 1974, p. 227.

13. Standage (1998).

14. David Hochfelder, *Partners in Crime: The Telegraph Industry, Finance Capitalism, and Organised Gambling, 1870–1920* IEEE History Centre, Rutgers University, 2001, http://www.ieeeghn.org/wiki/images/5/5b/Hochfelder.pdf

15. 'Ingenious fool Traps: Action taken Against Wall Street Swindlers,' *NY Times*, 8 October 1880, http://query.nytimes.com/gst/abstract.html?res=9907E1DC153FEE3ABC4053DFB667838B699FDE Accessible through 'download a high-resolution PDF' link.

16. Hochfelder, *Partners in Crime*.

17. Ibid.

18. Wesley MacNeil Oliver, 'Western Union, the American Federation of Labor, Google and the Changing Face of Privacy Advocates', *Mississippi Law Journal*, vol. 81, no. 5, 2012, pp. 971–990.

19. Bucket shops did however continue to operate illicitly in many state jurisdictions for some time.

20. Jonathan Lurie, *The Chicago Board of Trade, 1859–1905: The Dynamics of Self-Regulation* (Urbana, IL: University of Illinois Press, 1979) especially chapters 4 and 6. Fabian. Cited in Hochfelder *supra* note 16.

21. Foreign Relations of the United States, Paris Peace Conference, vol. IV, p. 226. Today cables are governed by traditional rules of jurisdiction deriving from their ownership, as well as by other aspects of international law, such as the Law of the Sea Convention and Article 54 of the Hague Regulations. See Michael N. Schmitt, *Tallinn Manual on the International Law Applicable to Cyber Warfare* (Cambridge: Cambridge University Press, 2013).

22. In this case a state grand jury issued a subpoena for all the telegrams sent between four named persons over a 15-month period. Western Union fought hard against such subpoenas incriminating its clients and couched in such general and sweeping terms, as it had in the earlier Babcock case (1876) and Entick v. Carrington (1877). This time, the Missouri Supreme Court accepted Western Union's position that the subpoena amounted to 'an indiscriminate search forbidden by the Constitution'.
23. MacNeil Oliver, 'Western Union, the American Federation of Labor, Google, and the Changing Face of Privacy Advocates', p. 981.
24. Ibid., p. 983.
25. According to court records, the extensive bootlegging network was the first of its kind involving some fifty employees, the use of sea vessels for transportation, underground storage facilities in Seattle and the upkeep of a central office 'equipped with executives, accountants, salesmen and a lawyer.'
26. Pikowsky observes that in the 1930s, the Supreme Court Congress interpreted the Telecommunications Act of 1934 to forbid wiretapping. Congress did not modify the statute to permit wiretapping until 1960. Robert A. Pikowsky, 'The Need for Revisions to the Law of Wiretapping and Interception of Email', *Michigan Telecommunications and Technology Law Review*, vol. 10, issue 1, Fall 2003, pp. 28–31. Cited in *supra* note 23.
27. Ibid.
28. "Katz v. United States." Oyez, 25 Jan. 2018, www.oyez.org/cases/1967/35.
29. This development led to the establishment of an Attorney General's Special Group on Organized Crime in the Department of Justice with regional offices from which intelligence information was gathered and grand jury proceedings conducted, concerning the Apalachin conferees. The Group's functions were later subsumed within the Department of Justice in a dedicated Organized Crime and Racketeering Section.
30. The Challenge of Crime in a Free Society: A Report by the President's Commission on Law Enforcement and Administration of Justice. Washington D.C. February, 1967. See in particular Chapter 7. https://www.ncjrs.gov/pdffiles1/nij/42.pdf.
31. Gotlieb, Dalfen & Katz, 'The Transborder Transfer of Information by Communications and Computer Systems: Issues and Approaches to Guiding Principles', p. 230.
32. Peter Gastrow, 'Penetrating State and Business: Organised Crime in Southern Africa', *Institute for Security Studies (ISS)*, vol. 2, 2003, pp. vii
33. President's Commission on Organized Crime, Interim Report to the President and the Attorney General: *The Cash Connection: Organized Crime, Financial Institutions, and Money Laundering,* October 1984, p. 8, https://www.ncjrs.gov/pdffiles1/Digitization/166517NCJRS.pdf.

34. S.Rep. No. 617, 91st Cong., 1st Sess. 76, 1969.
35. Interestingly, none of the IR literature of the time which focused on interdependence and transnational groups talks about transnational criminal actors.
36. Established by Executive Order 12435—President's Commission on Organized Crime. It ultimately led to the enactment of the Comprehensive Crime Control Act of 1984.
37. The 1983 Commission noted how mafia-connected persons such as Michele Sindona who made his fortune by laundering illicit funds through legitimate enterprise had "mastered the details of modern technology, international finance and foreign secrecy laws to create a select fraternity of money laundering professionals," with the result that organized crime was using banks and other financial institutions "as routinely, if not as frequently, as legitimate business." Again, restrictions on electronic surveillance (in respect of Forth Amendment rights) coupled with the growing complexity of transnational crime were alleged to have significantly enabled money laundering and weakened law enforcement responses.
38. The suggested amendments regarding wiretapping and the RFPA were included in Titles III and IV of the Cash Connection Report.
39. Remarks of the Attorney General before the President's Commission on Organized Crime, Washington D.C, 29 November, 1983 http://www.justice.gov/sites/default/files/ag/legacy/2011/08/23/11-29-1983.pdf.
40. Kelly White, *The Rise of Cyber Crime 1970 through 2010: A tour of the conditions that gave rise to cybercrime and the crimes themselves*, 2013 http://www.slideshare.net/bluesme/the-rise-of-cybercrime-1970s-2010-29879338.
41. DEA Drug Intelligence Report, 1997.
42. Melissa Hathaway, 'Connected Choices: How the Internet Is Challenging Sovereign Decisions', *American Foreign Policy Interests*, vol. 36, issue 5, November 2014, pp. 300–313.
43. Vivienne Jabri, *War and the Transformation of Global Politics*, 2nd edition (London and New York: Palgrave Macmillan, 2007 and 2010) p. 42.
44. The Changing Face of organized crime in New Jersey—A Status Report—State of New Jersey Commission of Investigation 2004 Report.
45. Ramesh Thakur and Jorge Heine, *The Dark Side of Globalization*. (United Nations University Press, 2011).
46. Misha Glenny, *McMafia: A Journey Through the Criminal Underground* (London: Vintage, 2009).
47. Gastrow, 'Penetrating State and Business: Organised Crime in Southern Africa', *supra* note 31.
48. The Cali Cartel: The New Kings of Cocaine. DEA Drug Intelligence Report, 1994.

49. See: 'UN Convention against Transnational Organized Crime and the Protocols Thereto' http://www.unodc.org/unodc/treaties/CTOC/.

50. The cases outlined in this chapter are based on desk research only, and are only indicative of how transnational crime avails of IT and cyber capabilities for force projection purposes.

51. As today, cellular phones were often bought in bulk allowing criminal entrepreneurs shift quickly from one phone to another and outwitting law enforcement. As for digital pagers, these were generally used to transmit coded messages regarding meeting venues, changes to delivery schedules etc. Pagers were difficult to surveil, and according to the DEA, paging services often 'tipped off'.

52. DEA Drug Intelligence Report, 1994.

53. DEA Drug Intelligence Report, 1997.

54. DEA Drug Intelligence Report, 1994.

55. Ibid.

56. David Lane, *Into the Heart of the Mafia: A Journey Through the Italian South*. (Profile Books LTD 2010) p. 72.

57. Red Herring: Law Enforcement's 'Going Dark Spiel' *The Journal of Electronic Surveillance Technology*, 6 February, 2015 https://insidersuveillance.com/red-herring-law-enforcements-going-dark-spiel/

58. 50 U.S.C. 1701–1706.

59. 60 FR 54579, 24 October 1995.

60. Section 1 of the Order blocks, with certain exceptions, all property and interests in property that are in the United States, or that hereafter come within the United States or that are or hereafter come within the possession or control of United States persons, of: (1) The persons listed in an Annex to the Order; (2) any foreign person determined by the Secretary of Treasury, in consultation with the Attorney General and Secretary of State, to play a significant role in international narcotics trafficking centered in Colombia; or (3) to materially assist in, or provide financial or technological support for or goods or services in support of, the narcotics trafficking activities of persons designated in or pursuant to this order; and (4) persons determined by the Secretary of the Treasury, in consultation with the Attorney General and the Secretary of State, to be owned or controlled by, or to act for or on behalf of, persons designated pursuant to this Order.

61. The latter included firms such as CALI @ TELE.COM LTDA. (a.k.a. HOLA TELECOMUNICACIONES and COMUNICACIONES ABIERTAS CAMARY LTDA. These companies were fronts for the Norte del Valle cartel, operating under the name of Piedad Rocio Sanchez Candelo, a member of the Grajales family, one of the key members of the cartel. See: El Pais, 28 November 2006, https://www.federalregister.gov/articles/2006/12/01/E6-20375/additional-

designation-of-persons-pursuant-to-executive-order-12978#h-4 Dept. of Treasury). According to the Department of Treasury, Sanchez Candelo was removed from the SDN list in 2012.

62. Rubén Luis Ayala, 'La Marina arresta a fundador de Los Zetas 'Lucky' y desconecta las comunicaciones del cartel', *Agora*, December 2011, http://amigosdetamaulipas2.mforos.com/1832982/10431860-la-marina-desconecta-las-comunicaciones-del-cartel/.

63. Damon Tabor, *Radio Tecnico: How the Zetas Cartel Took Over Mexico with Walkie-Talkies*, posted 25 March, 2014 http://www.popsci.com/article/technology/radio-tecnico-how-zetas-cartel-took-over-mexico-walkie-talkies; FoxNews (Latino), December 2011, Drug Cartels in Mexico Have a Clandestine National radio Network.

64. Fox News, 2011.

65. Ibid.

66. See United Nations, 'Report of the independent expert on minority issues. Addendum: Mission to Guyana' (28 July to 1 August, 2008), Human Rights Council, A/HRC/10/11/Add.2, 27 February 2009.

67. Other weapons and equipment included M-16 assault rifles with night vision devices, an Uzi sub-machine gun with silencer, Glock 9mm pistols, a 12-gauge shotgun, other small caliber weapons, bullet-proof vests and helmets.

68. The company's co-director, Peter Myers, testified that the cellular intercept equipment found in Khan's possession was indeed sold directly to him. The testimony was actually provided in the trial of Khan's attorney, Roger Simels who himself was on trial for plotting to kill a witness against Khan. Two computers belonging to Simels connecting Khan to the surveillance equipment were discovered.

69. US Diplomatic Cable: *Blaze at Ministry of Health is Out, But New Allegations Keep Fires Burning*, 09GEORGETOWN18_a. [Accessed 9 March, 2015].

70. Kavanagh et al., Getting Smart and Scaling Up: Responding to the Impact of Organized Crime on Governance in Developing Countries, 7 June 2013. See Summer Walker, pp. 198–216, for the specific case study on Guyana. http://cic.nyu.edu/content/responding-impact-organised-crime-governance-developing-countries.

71. See for example, Exec. Order 13606 of April 2012 'Blocking the Property and Suspending Entry Into the United States of Certain Persons With Respect to Grave Human Rights Abuses by the Governments of Iran and Syria via Information Technology'.

72. According to a 2012 report, in Iran, firms controlled by the Revolutionary Guard have acquired large stakes in key economic sectors, including telecommunications, where sanctions have forced global companies to

abandon some projects to IRGC-linked companies. The report notes that the longer sanctions persist, the more economic transactions will be controlled by the Iranian leadership through black-market channels.

See: *Weighing Benefits and Costs of International Sanctions against Iran*, The Iran Project, 2012 http://bakerinstitute.org/files/1339/.

73. Internet Facilitated Organised Crime Threat Assessment (iOCTA) (2014), EC3, EUROPOL Cybercrime Center.

74. Ibid, p. 11.

75. After Rotterdam, Antwerp is Europe's largest port. In 2010, some 8.468.476 containers passed through the Port of Antwerp. The sheer quantity of goods passing through the port makes searching them one by one impossible. Customs aim to screen 2% of all declared goods, using scanners and other devices, but even that goal has proved over ambitious, hence it is impossible to discern the scale of illegal trafficking. Frans Van Rompuy, director-general of the (Belgian) Federal Governmental Department for Mobility assumes that "between 100 and 1,000 containers annually contain illegal trafficked goods. This is ... an estimation, reliable figures are not available." Whereas Rotterdam is renowned for its Far East connections, Antwerp is a typical trans-Atlantic port. Out of 8.5 million containers, some 948.597 came from North or Central America and some 281.241 from South-America. See: Kristof Clerix, 'The Port of Antwerp is a honey jar for organized crime', *Mondial Nieuws*, 31 August 2011, http://www.mo.be/node/8041

76. Communication with case officer, 7 April 2015.

77. Ibid.

78. Ibid.

79. During the joint operation, Dutch and Belgian police are reported to have seized six firearms including a machine gun and silencer, bulletproof vests, and 1.3m euros (£1.1m) in cash inside a suitcase.

80. Communication with case officer, 7 April 2015.

81. For a deeper insight into the range of cybersecurity risks at sea, see for example: Proceedings of the Marine Safety & Security Council. *The Coastguard Journal of Safety & Security at Sea*, winter 2014–2015, http://www.uscg.mil/proceedings/archive/2014/Vol71_No4_Wint2014.pdf.

82. See: Scott Helfstein, Scott with John Solomon, *Risky Business: The Global Threat Network and the Politics of Contraband*, (Combating Terrorism Centre at West Point, May 2014) https://www.ctc.usma.edu/v2/wp-content/uploads/2014/05/RiskyBusiness_final.pdf.

83. 'The Spider and the Web: The Fog of War Descends on Cyberspace', *The Economist*, 24 September 2011. In 2010 alone, five newspapers admitted in print that due to the risks to their reporters, they would stop covering sensitive drug-war stories.

84. 'Gang Sends Message with Blogger Beheading', *The Houston Chronicle*, 10 November 2011, http://www.chron.com/news/nation-world/article/Gang-sends-message-with-blogger-beheading-2260814.php.

85. Tamaulipas Tuitera, 'Blogger Kidnapped and Killed', *Borderland Beat*, 16 October 2014, http://www.borderlandbeat.com/2014/10/vxt-blogger-kidnapped-and-killed.html.

86. Jorge Luis Sierra, 'Digital and Mobile Security for Mexican Journalists and Bloggers: Results of a Survey of Mexican journalists and bloggers', *Freedom House* and the *International Center for Journalists*.

87. Ibid.

88. Geoffrey Ramsey, 'Update: Anonymous Vs. the Zetas', *Borderland Beat*, 1 November 2011, http://www.borderlandbeat.com/2011/11/anonymous-vs-zetas-battle-continues.html.

89. 'Anonymous cancela #OpCartel por amenazas', *El Universal*, 4 Novembre 2011.

90. 'The Spider and the Web: The Fog of War Descends on Cyberspace'.

91. In a 2013 report, Robert Muggah and Gustavo Diniz highlight the different types of approaches to how ICTs are being used for the purpose of violence prevention in the Americas. The typology set includes: vertical (government-government); vertical (government-citizen); horizontal (citizen-government); and horizontal (citizen-citizen) approaches. See Robert Muggah and Gustavo Diniz, 'Digitally Enhanced Violence Prevention in the Americas', *Stability: International Journal of Security and Development,* vol. 2, Issue 3, 2013 https://doi.org/10.5334/sta.cq.

92. The study was conducted by Gareth Owen, University of Portsmouth computer science researcher and presented at the Chaos Computer Congress in Hamburg, Germany on 30 December 2014.

93. See: The extent to which the latter refers to transnational or organized crime is unclear, and an on-going debate regarding the methodology of the study has ensued. See for example: 'No, Department of Justice, 80% of Tor traffic is Not Child Porn', *Wired*, 1 January 2015, http://www.wired.com/2015/01/department-justice-80-percent-tor-traffic-child-porn/.

94. U.S. Attorney's Office, *Ross Ulbricht, the Creator and Owner of the Silk Road Website, Found Guilty in Manhattan Federal Court on All Counts,* Southern District of New York, 5 February 2015.

95. According to the complaint, the site also sold hacking tools, such as keystroke loggers, password crackers and remote access and banking Trojans, as well as access to hacked Amazon and Netflix accounts and teaching tools such as a tutorial describing "22 different methods" for hacking ATMs. It also marketed a "Blackmarket Contact List", which provided handy contact information for hit men available for hire in more than ten countries, or purveyors of counterfeit bills and firearms. *Wired* http://www.wired.com/2013/10/silk-road-raided/.

96. *United States of America v. Ross William Ulbricht*, 14 CRIM 068, 4 February 2014, http://www.justice.gov/usao/nys/pressreleases/February14/RossUlbrichtIndictmentPR/US%20v.%20Ross%20Ulbricht%20Indictment.pdf.
97. Kevin Pulsen, 'In Las Vegas Courtroom, First Ever Cybercrime RICO Trial Begins', *Wired*, 20 November 2013, http://www.wired.com/2013/11/open-market-trial-begins/.
98. Ibid.
99. Fran Berkman, 'Silk Road Reborn: There's a New Dread Pirate Roberts', *Mashable UK*, 6 November 2013, http://mashable.com/2013/11/06/silk-road-dread-pirate-roberts/.
100. Ibid.
101. Ibid. See also Pierluigi Paganini, 'The Evolution of Black Markets after Operation Onymous', *Security Affairs*, 26 November 2014, http://securityaffairs.co/wordpress/30538/cyber-crime/evolution-black-market.html.
102. Operation Onymous, implemented in November 2014 by law enforcement and judicial agencies from around the globe was coordinated by the European Cybercrime Center (EC3) and is considered a milestone in the fight against underground black markets.
103. James B. Comey, Director FBI, *Going Dark: Are Technology, Privacy and Public Safety on a Collision Course?*, Brookings Institution, Washington DC 16 October 2014, http://www.fbi.gov/news/speeches/going-dark-are-technology-privacy-and-public-safety-on-a-collision-course.
104. For example, members of the terrorist group found one of the hotel guests hiding in a suite. In order to determine his identity they took a photo, sent it directly to the operations cell which then googled the image, discovering that the person was not a school teacher as he claimed to be, but rather the second wealthiest man in India. The order from the operations cell was to "kill him." Marc Goodman: *A Vision of Crimes in the Future*, Ted Talks, Edinburgh, June 2012.
105. 'China wants cyber crime suspects extradited', *NTV Kenya*, uploaded on 11 January 2015, https://www.youtube.com/watch?v=9P37Oa5n3W8.
106. Fredrick Nzwili, 'China and Kenya at odds over suspected Chinese cyber criminals', *The Christian Science Monitor*, 26 January 2015, http://www.csmonitor.com/World/Africa/2015/0126/China-and-Kenya-at-odds-over-suspected-Chinese-cyber-criminals.
107. Ndegwa Muhoro, director of Kenya's Criminal Investigations Department, cited in '77 Chinese Nationals Arrested in Kenya for Cybercrimes', *Newsweek*, 5 December 2014, http://europe.newsweek.com/77-chinese-nationals-arrested-kenya-cybercrimes-289539.
108. South China Morning Post. 'Beijing defends deportation of Taiwan crime suspects to mainland China'. 22 February 2017.

109. United Nations: 'The Road to Dignity by 2030: Ending Poverty, Transforming All Lives and Protecting the Planet: Synthesis Report of the Secretary-General on the Post-2015 Sustainable Development Agenda', A/69/700 of 4 December 2014.

110. See SDG 16: "Promote peaceful and inclusive societies for sustainable development, provide access to justice for all and build effective, accountable and inclusive institutions at all levels" and more specifically the 16.4 target: "By 2030 significantly reduce illicit financial and arms flows, strengthen recovery and return of stolen assets, and combat all forms of organised crime." Open Working Group proposal for Sustainable Development Goals http://sustainabledevelopment.un.org/sdgsproposal.html. For a more detailed overview of how crime impacts on governance in developing countries see: Kavanagh et al., *supra* note 69; and the Global Initiative on Transnational Organized Crime (2015), Organised Crime: A Cross-Cutting Threat to Sustainable Development.

111. In addition to organized crime and illicit trade, the inability to efficiently govern results from corruption, the presence of impunity and generally weak rule of law. The report also notes that over past years, the links between many forms of global crime and corruption and their impact on global security, extremism, terrorism and fragile states have only grown stronger, and it is critical to acknowledge and address them through more effective policies that curb illegal financial flows, foster transparent governance and build capacity around anti-crime efforts at the national and local levels. See: http://www3.weforum.org/docs/WEF_Global_Risks_2015_Report15.pdf.

112. The Global Risks Report 2014. World Economic Forum.

113. One of the more controversial provisions of which was to broaden the surveillance powers of federal law enforcement officials, allowing investigators to conduct searches without informing the target of the search. The broad provision was initially aimed at suspected terrorists but was discovered to be used 'as an every day investigative tool'.

114. Red Herring: Law Enforcement's 'Going Dark Spiel'.

115. In 1999, and in a case involving crime boss Nicky Scarfo, FBI agents used a key-logger system to search for encryption keys on Scarfoag PC and find passwords that provided access to hidden files on illegal gambling another illicit activities.

116. Legal authorities to use malware can also be found in Title III of the Omnibus Crime Bill, the Foreign Intelligence Service Act (FISA) and the Electronic Communications Privacy Act (ECPA). Red Herring: Law Enforcement's 'Going Dark Spiel', *supra* note 54.

117. For an excellent insight into the question of policing and technology see: Evgeny Morozov, *To Save Everything, Click Here: Technology, Solutionism*

and the Urge to Solve Problems that Don't Exist (London: Penguin Books, 2013), Chapter Six, Less Crime, More Punishment.

118. 'Privacy and Security: A Modern and transparent legal framework', *Intelligence and Security Committee of Parliament*, 12 March 2015, http://bit.ly/1UuCnL3.

119. 'Toward a Social Compact for Digital Privacy and Security: Statement by the Global Commission on Internet Governance', *Centre for International Governance Innovation (CIGI)* and *Chatham House*, April 2015, https://ourinternet-files.s3.amazonaws.com/publications/GCIG_Social_Compact.pdf.

120. Marc Goodman, *Future Crimes: Everything is Connected, Everyone is Vulnerable and What We Can Do About It*, (New York: Knopf Doubleday Publishing Group, 2015).

121. A renewed focus on MLATs has emerged in the past months, provoked in part by the absence of a global framework to respond to cybercrime. See in particular: 'Data Beyond Borders: Mutual Legal Assistance in the Internet Age', *Global Network Initiative*, January 2015, https://globalnetworkinitiative.org/sites/default/files/GNI%20MLAT%20Report.pdf.

122. See Morozov, *To Save Everything, Click Here: Technology, Solutionism and the Urge to Solve Problems that Don't Exist*, *supra* note 115.

123. Helfstein with Solomon, *Risky Business: The Global Threat Network and the Politics of Contraband*.

124. U.S. submission to the 2014–2015 Group of Governmental Experts.

125. For example, through companies such as VUPEN security or The Hacking Team.

126. See for example: John B. Sheldon, 'Geopolitics and Cyber Power: Why Geography Still Matters', *American Foreign Policy Interests: The Journal of the National Committee on American Foreign Policy*, vol. 36, issue 5, 2014; David Kilcullen, *Out of the Mountains: The Coming of Age of the Urban Guerrilla*, (Oxford: Oxford University Press 2013).

127. Sheldon, 'Geopolitics and Cyber Power: Why Geography Still Matters'.

CHAPTER 4

Measuring Illicit Trade and Its Wider Impact

Karl Lallerstedt

Abstract Illicit trade is a broad and varied collection of phenomena requiring a broad palette of coordinated policy responses. But unlike the threat of terrorism, which produces highly visible incidents, most of the times illicit trade remains below the surface, impeding the mobilisation of the prerequisite political will to address the threat. These challenges underline the need for better data to quantify and assess the impact of illicit trade, in order to empower policymakers to gauge their policy response more appropriately.

Keywords Illicit trade • Corruption • Illicit financial flows • Smuggling • Border (as in border control and border security)

Illicit trade is arguably the lifeblood of organized crime and the need to better understand this phenomenon and its strategic impact is gaining increasing traction in policy circles, as indicated by the establishment of the Task Force on Countering Illicit Trade, launched by the Organisation for Economic Co-operation and Development (OECD) in 2013.[1] Yet, this is far from being an easy endeavour. The multifaceted and covert nature of

K. Lallerstedt (✉)
The Global Initiative Against Transnational Organized Crime,
Geneva, Switzerland

© The Author(s) 2018
V. Comolli (ed.), *Organized Crime and Illicit Trade*,
https://doi.org/10.1007/978-3-319-72968-8_4

illicit trade complicates the analysis which, in turn, underpins the design of effective policy.

What is clear, however, is that the overall negative impact of illicit trade far exceeds the sum of its constituent parts. Despite the synergistic relationship between different forms of illicit trade it is frequently addressed as separate categories, such as narcotics, excise goods or counterfeit goods.

In this context, this chapter provides a holistic overview of the scale and impact of the illicit trade mega-problem, highlighting the challenges of measuring the problem as exemplified by several studies and surveys that have been launched internationally to quantify the size of the different forms of illicit trade and the costs associated with it. The chapter concludes with some considerations on how to achieve more policy relevant analysis and how to improve the way measurements are conducted.

Before embarking on this discussion it is worth reflecting on definitions. In fact, similarly to 'organized crime', of which criminologist Klaus von Lampe has compiled some 190 definitions,[2] illicit trade can also be defined in different ways. Adopting a simple and pragmatic approach, if a given form of trade is illegal in a particular jurisdiction then it can be classified as illicit. This would mean that trade in prohibited products, such as certain narcotics, will always constitute illicit trade. But generic medication, or marijuana, when sold in jurisdictions where they are legal would not constitute illicit trade.

Most *transnational* organized crime activity would constitute illicit trade, whereas purely *domestic* organized crime activity such as extortion, public contracts manipulation and thefts would not. Some narcotics, counterfeit and illicit environmental trade also remains purely *domestic*, although the major flows are transnational. The World Customs Organisation (WCO) offers some help:

> Illicit trade involves money, goods or value gained from illegal and otherwise unethical activity. It encompasses a variety of illegal trading activities, including human trafficking, environmental crime, illegal trade in natural resources, intellectual property infringements, trade in certain substances that cause health or safety risks, smuggling of excisable goods, trade in illegal drugs, and a variety of illicit financial flows.[3]

THE SCALE OF THE PROBLEM

One commonality between all forms of illicit trade is that they constitute criminal activity. Gathering statistics to quantify such phenomena is not a straight forward exercise. Furthermore key actors with insights into illicit trade—namely law enforcement agencies, intelligence agencies, and the private enterprises and individuals affected—are understandably reluctant to share their insights openly. These intrinsic challenges make an accurate measurement of many aspects of illicit trade more or less impossible, forcing analysts to rely on rough estimates, proxy measures, and best guesstimates. Despite these limitations a number of more or less controversial estimates of the value of various flows have been made, making it clear that illicit trade is a significant part of the global economy.

A United Nations Office on Drugs and Crime (UNODC) meta study estimated the global turnover of transnational organized crime at US$870 billion in 2009, representing 1.5% of global gross domestic product (GDP), close to 7% of global merchandise trade, and six times official global development assistance budgets. Three of the largest contributing subcomponents used by the UNODC were narcotics (US$320bn), counterfeits (US$250bn), and human trafficking (US$32bn).[4] Although this UNODC study has not been received without criticism, using its estimate and accounting for economic growth and inflation the annual total turnover of transnational organized crime could now be expected to exceed US$1 trillion.

A 2012 OECD study estimated the value of international environmental crime, which includes illegal trade in wildlife; illegal logging and its associated timber trade; illegal, unreported, and unregulated (IUU) fishing; illegal trade in controlled chemicals (particularly in ozone-depleting substances); and illegal disposal of hazardous waste, at US$30–70bn.[5] Another big category of illicit trade is the contraband trade in excise goods such as tobacco, alcohol and petroleum products. A 2010 paper by illicit tobacco expert Luk Joossens estimated that 11.6% of global tobacco consumption was illicit, resulting in tax losses exceeding US$40bn.[6] The World Health Organization (WHO)'s *Global Status Report on Alcohol & Health 2014* estimated that 25% of global alcohol consumption was unrecorded (homemade alcohol, illegally produced or sold outside normal government controls).[7]

Irrespective of the potential shortcomings of the aforementioned UNODC meta-study it would appear clear that the trade in narcotics and counterfeit goods are the two largest categories of illicit trade. The estimate for the latter of the two comes from a 2009 OECD study based on extrapolations from customs seizure data and trade data. A more recent OECD study estimated that the value of internationally traded pirated and counterfeit goods in 2013 represented up to 2.5 percent of world trade, or US$461.[8] This would make counterfeits the single largest category of illicitly traded goods.

The 2015 survey on losses suffered by Japanese companies due to counterfeiting conducted by the Japanese Patent Office indicated that 21.9% of responding companies were affected.[9] Unfortunately most countries do not conduct similar assessments, hence it is not possible to have a comparable global picture.

Law enforcement seizures illustrate that counterfeiting is not just about fake handbags and sunglasses. In 2014 Interpol press releases reported a number of law enforcement operation seizures illustrating the variety and scale of the problem. One operation netted 1,200 tonnes of counterfeit or substandard food products and 430,000 litres of counterfeit drinks.[10] An operation focusing on a single factory resulted in the seizure of US$37m worth of fake cosmetics containing high levels of mercury, and 589 arrests.[11]

Another example is Operation Biyela, a ten day operation coordinated by the WCO covering 23 African countries in 2013, which netted over a billion illicit products. They included over 550m pharmaceutical products ranging from antibiotics to HIV/AIDS treatment. Over 450m fake electronic appliances, over 31m food items, 16m transportation and spare parts, and over 14m other items including insecticides were also intercepted in the same operation.[12]

IMPACT OF ILLICIT TRADE

At first glance, even a figure such as the UNODC estimate that the turnover of transnational organized crime is equivalent to 1.5% of global GDP may not seem that shocking. But the total impact is far more significant if one takes into account the negative impact and repercussions that these activities have. Specifically, illicit trade impacts on global security in six major ways:

- It is a source of income for criminal non-state actors;
- It has corrosive effect on governance;

- It undermines border security;
- It endangers public health;
- It contributes to the depletion of environmental resources and permanently damages ecosystems;
- It causes significant economic costs.

The following pages will focus on these key impacts while acknowledging that there are other, second-tier, repercussions of which one should not lose sight. For example, the illicit arms trade, estimated at US$170–320m[13] per year by the UNODC, may not be so significant in terms of monetary turn-over, but the weapons remain operational for decades and have a significant impact by serving as empowerment tools for criminal non-state actors.

Income for Organized Crime, Terrorists, and Warring Parties

"It's the Economy, Stupid"

Any enterprise requires money to operate, even when the business is organized crime, terrorism or insurgency. The fundamental driver behind illicit trade is the revenue it generates for the entities involved.

In the European Union alone there were more than 5,000 international organized crime groups under investigation in 2017, around 45 percent of which are generating revenues from multiple forms of criminal activities.[14,15] Consequently, even less politically prioritised forms of illicit trade can empower organisations involved in criminal activities of greater concern. To cite one example, referring to counterfeits, Interpol has stated the "[a] clear link has been established between the trafficking of illicit goods and transnational organized crime" and that "[t]hey use the profits to fund other criminal activities such as drug trafficking, people smuggling and robbery."[16]

It is not only organized crime groups who generate revenue from illicit trade. Global demand for narcotics has financed terrorists and insurgent groups such as in the case of cocaine financing Colombia's Fuerzas Armadas Revolucionarias de Colombia (FARC)[17] or heroin contributing to an income stream for the Taliban.[18] The often-cited Mokhtar Belmokhtar—the al-Qaida affiliated mastermind behind the 2013 In-Amenas gas plant hostage taking in Algeria resulting in over 60 deaths—has also been dubbed "Mr Marlboro" due to his profiteering on tobacco smuggling across the Sahel.[19] Somalia's Al-Shabaab has profited from the illegal trade in commodities as mundane as sugar and charcoal.[20] The so-called Islamic State of Iraq and al-Sham (ISIS) has generated revenues through a host of different forms of illicit trade activities ranging from oil, antiquities, human smuggling and consumer goods.[21] Virtually all well-known terrorist organisations are known to have profited from some form of illicit trade.

Similarly, any form of military power needs to be sustained by an economic base. Research by James Fearon at Stanford University suggests that the income from illicit trade can play a major role in prolonging civil wars. Fearon assessed historic civil war data and found that the average duration of civil wars with major reliance on contraband trade was 48.2 years, versus 8.8 years for conflicts that were not sustained by contraband trade.[22]

Corrosive Effect on Governance

Corruption undermines governance, democracy and the rule of law. As illicit trade generates significant profits for the parties involved, yet exposes them to risk, efforts to buy 'insurance' or 'protection' from government officials, law enforcement and politicians will occur, perverting governance in the process. Sometimes the corruption goes beyond criminal co-option of public officials and private sector actors, with leading individuals within the state apparatus benefiting more directly from illicit trade. The degree of criminal influence varies, with Moisés Naím coining the term 'mafia states' to describe the extreme end of the spectrum of states serving criminal interests.[23]

Vidar Helgessen, the former Secretary General of the International Institute for Democracy and Electoral Assistance (International IDEA), wrote in 2013 that

> the world is witnessing a growing threat from transnational illicit networks to the legitimacy of democratic institutions and political processes in both emerging and established democracies.
>
> Transnational organized crime networks exist in countries with a long tradition of institutional development, such as Colombia, as well as in countries which are fragile, such as Guatemala or Haiti. They exist in post-communist countries, now members of the European Union (EU), such as the Baltic states and Romania. They exist in relatively new democracies in

West Africa, and in well-established democracies, such as Italy. They may lead to the effective takeover of states by illicit drug networks, controlling political institutions, political parties and candidates—and, in the process, obliterating the voices and demands of ordinary people.[24]

As in the theory of 'trickle-down economics', the effects of corruption reach beyond the initial beneficiary. The 2011 World Bank report *Crime and Violence in Central America: A Development Challenge* suggests that the corruption associated with illicit trade undermines the rule of law more broadly:

> Existing evidence indicates that drug trafficking increases corruption levels in the criminal justice systems of some Central American countries and tarnishes the legitimacy of state institutions in the public's mind. On average, victims of crime tend to: (i) have less trust in the criminal justice system; (ii) support taking the law into their own hands in larger numbers; and (iii) believe less strongly that the rule of law should always be respected.[25]

Rather than focus on the details of how this 'trickling down' affects governance let us focus on a few illustrative examples of illicit trade interplay with the highest powers of state.

The president of Paraguay, Horacio Cartes, is also owner of Grupo Cartes, which includes the country's largest cigarette manufacturer, Tabacalera del Este (Tabesa). Tabesa's cigarettes are the most smuggled in Latin America.[26] Looking at illicit tobacco alone there are other examples where the role of states or political elites can be questioned. Industry sources and defectors allege that North Korea has been involved in extensive production of counterfeit cigarettes,[27] a command economy where little activity is likely to occur without high-level endorsement. Cigarettes manufactured by Belarusian state owned enterprises have been heavily smuggled into European markets.[28] Savanna Tobacco in Zimbabwe, where a relative of former President Mugabe is a major shareholder, has been accused of tobacco smuggling into South Africa.[29] Amalgamated Tobacco Manufacturers in South Africa, where President Zuma's son Edward is a shareholder, was investigated by the South African Revenue Services due to suspicions of involvement in the illicit tobacco trade.[30]

The narcotics trade abounds with illustrative cases of high level involvement and corruption. Guinea Bissau has become well known for its role in cocaine trafficking. In 2013 the former head of Guinea Bissau's Navy,

Rear Admiral Jose Americo Bubo Na Tchuto, was apprehended in international waters and transferred to the US where he was charged with conspiring to distribute cocaine.[31] In 2006 two Latin Americans were detained in Guinea-Bissau while in possession of 670kg of cocaine—but the army secured their release and the cocaine vanished.[32] In Afghanistan, the world's leading supplier of opium, the former president's brother and chairman of the Kandahar Provincial Council, Ahmed Wali Karzai (who was killed in 2011) was fingered by international media for involvement in the country's drugs trade.[33]

The trade in counterfeit goods is not exempt from high level complicity. Representatives of leading corporations have expressed serious concern over high level political complicity in the trade of counterfeit goods, as well as the political 'shielding' of perpetrators in developing countries.[34]

The problem of corruption and criminal complicity at the very highest levels of political power is not limited to the developing world. In 2014 the Italian Supreme Court upheld that Marcello Dell'Utri, one of former Prime Minister Silvio Berlusconi's closest business partners and political allies, as well as co-founder of Berlusconi's Forza Italia party, was guilty of complicity in conspiracy with the Sicilian Mafia.[35] The court found that "for 18 years, from 1974 to 1992, Marcello Dell'Utri was the guarantor of the agreement between Berlusconi and Cosa Nostra". Berlusconi himself could not be tried due the 20-year statute of limitations for mafia-related offences.[36]

Russia is another example of a country with a seemingly symbiotic relationship between the most powerful individuals within the state and organized crime. In 2015, at the inquiry into the death of the former Russian spy Alexander Litvinenko in London nine years earlier, the Queen's Counsel representing the widow of Mr Litvinenko claimed that

> the intimate relationship that will be shown to exist between the Kremlin and Russian organised crime syndicates are so close as to make the two effectively indistinguishable," and that "the startling truth, which is going to be revealed in public by the evidence in this inquiry, is that a significant part of the Russian organised crime around the world is organised directly from the office of the Kremlin. Vladimir Putin's Russia is a mafia state.[37]

Mr Emmerson represented one side in the hearing, and as such may not be considered entirely objective, but he is certainly not alone in claiming there exists an intimate Kremlin-mafia relationship.

The ongoing conflict in the eastern Ukraine raises the question of whether organized crime has served as a Russian foreign policy instrument. Professor Mark Galeotti from New York University has pointed out that

> Many of the burly and well-armed 'self-defense volunteers' who came out on the streets alongside the not-officially-Russian troops turned out to be local gangsters, and the governing elite there have close, long-term relations with organized crime. Likewise, in eastern Ukraine, criminals have been sworn in as members of local militias and even risen to senior ranks, while the police, long known for their corruption, are fighting alongside them.[38]

With organized crime's ability to corrupt, intimidate, and mobilise violence, the global reach of Russian organized crime networks, particularly in the former Soviet space, provides the Kremlin with a potential tool to influence and destabilise.

Undermining Border Security

Border security is undermined both by the corruption of state officials and organized crime's efforts to physically bypass border controls. In addition to organized crime groups, states and terrorists also have interests in evading border security.

Corruption

The arrest of Juan Carlos Ramírez Abadía, one of the leaders of the Norte del Valle Cartel in Colombia, shed some light on how corruption serves as a tool enabling narco-traffickers to operate with impunity. His seized computer indicated that between 2003 and 2006 there were three admirals, seven army and police colonels, and two naval captains on his payroll. Corrupt officials would move ships to allow the transportation of narcotics and leaked details of naval patrols. At the same time they made sure that what Ramírez Abadía called 'intelligent highways' were in place. These consisted of favorable routes for convoys carrying cocaine or the precursors used to process the coca base along which patrols were no longer carried out by the army or the police specifically to facilitate this illicit trafficking.[39]

The extent and cost of the bribing that took place was significant. It was believed that in 2004, he was paying monthly bribes amounting to

USD$4m disbursed to officials from the Administrative Department of Security, the police, the army, the Public Prosecutor's Office, the justice system, the National Registry Office, the Agustín Codazzi Geographic Institute, the National Penitentiary Institute and the media. Purchased favours ranged from amending witness statements to dismantling a checkpoint, from producing forged identity documents to allowing the transit of a consignment of coca. At the end of the year Ramírez Abadía even paid an end-of-year bonus of almost US$3m to the government officials on his payroll.[40]

Colombia's most important Pacific port, Buenaventura, seemed to be completely corrupted by the narco-traffickers with studies suggesting that "the local authorities, dock workers, port officials and ship crews are all involved, along with young unemployed people who risk their lives to place the drugs where their contacts tell them."[41]

Narco-corruption in Colombia may be extreme, but corruption is a global concern. A study carried out by the Centre for the Study of Democracy, commissioned by the European Border Agency Frontex, illustrates how vulnerable EU borders are to corruption.[42] The numbers of EU member states confirming border guard involvement in a range of illicit activities over a three year period are listed in the Table 4.1 below.

In 2010, 136 EU border guards were prosecuted for corrupt activities, but this figure understates the problem. In Romania, 510 were under suspicion during that year alone.[43] Corruption is not limited to the narrow sector of border security officials. And the true extent of corruption will never be known as the exposed cases are only the tip of the iceberg.

Physical Evasion

In addition to undermining border security through corruption, sophisticated technical methods are also employed by organized crime to avoid state interception efforts. One example is the 700 meter long tunnel equipped with its own narrow-gauge railway under the Slovak-Ukrainian border, discovered in 2012. Law enforcement officials seized millions of cigarettes in the operation, but it could have been used to smuggle other goods as well as people.[44] Sophisticated tunnels to facilitate smuggling across borders have been discovered in several locations, of which the best known are across the US-Mexico border[45] and from the Gaza strip.[46]

The use of drones is another method of avoiding detection. In 2014 an autonomous aircraft carrying a 10kg cargo of contraband cigarettes was detained by the Russian Federal Security Service (FSB). In this case, the

Table 4.1 Number of EU member states identifying border guard involvement in corrupt activities: Survey of border guards and internal affairs units

Corrupt activities	Detected cases, or not detected but known to exist (2007–2010)
Illegally providing information to criminal groups	13
Illegally providing information to migrants	13
Trafficking in cigarettes	15
Smuggling of other consumer goods (oil, alcohol)	13
Smuggling of stolen vehicles	12
Trafficking in drugs	10
Smuggling of irregular immigrants	12
Appointing individuals connected to organized crime	8
Facilitating illegal work/stay of immigrants	12
Other contraband (firearms)	9
Trafficking in human beings	10
Petty corruption (small bribes) related to facilitation of smuggling	13
Allowing the entry/exit of individuals who are on 'wanted' lists/ have travel ban	10

Confirmed cases or not detected but known to exist, survey of border guards and internal affairs units for period 2007–2010. Ibid.

drone's operators were smuggling cigarettes from Russia to Lithuania, but the craft could also have been used to carry other goods.[47] In 2015, a drone carrying 3kg of crystal meth crashed near the Mexican border in California.[48]

Perhaps the most extreme application of technology to evade border controls came to light after the Colombian Navy's 2011 seizure of a 'homemade' 31-metre fibreglass submarine capable of reaching Mexico, with space for a crew of four and an eight-tonne cargo.[49] In 2013 frogmen were apprehended in Rotterdam, Europe's busiest port, with underwater propulsion devices and inflatable parachutes, planning to remove a 'narco-torpedo' with over 100kg of cocaine attached to a ship's hull.[50]

States

Organized crime groups are not alone in wishing to evade border controls, states may share this interest. In 2014 Iranian President Hassan Rouhani stated on national television: "Of course we bypass sanctions. We are proud that we bypass sanctions because the sanctions are illegal."[51] Iran has both supplied weapons[52] and obtained dual use technology potentially useful in developing weapons of mass destruction by leveraging illicit transportation networks.[53]

States may not only wish to evade border controls to bypass sanctions, but to profiteer on illicit trade. On North Korea, Douglas Lovelace, Director of the Strategic Studies Institute at the US Army War College has argued that North Korea's Central Committee Bureau 39 had an active role in the region's criminal economy with tentacles extending well beyond Asia and that included activities such as narcotics trafficking, money laundering, counterfeiting and cigarette smuggling.[54] Specifically, it is believed that Pyongyang has used its naval vessels and merchant fleet, as well as its diplomatic corps, to deliver drugs and other illicit goods to organized crime groups abroad. One of the more high profile incidents was when the Japanese Coast Guard sank a North Korean Naval vessel operated by Special Forces intending to deliver methamphetamines to the Japanese Yakuza.[55]

Terrorists

Like rogue states and organized crime groups, terrorists also have an interest in bypassing border controls. Of particular concern is that the extensive human smuggling industry can facilitate the movement of terrorists across borders. In the record year 2015, over 1.2 million persons applied for asylum in the European Union,[56] and many others entered seeking to live an undeclared existence. A large number of migrants employ the services of human smugglers which has created a mass industry for moving large numbers of people clandestinely into the continent. Already before the European 2015 'refuge crisis' had started journalist Mike Giglio raised the alarm that ISIS had smuggled jihadis, masking as refugees, into Europe using the services of human smugglers.[57]

Harming Public Health

Narcotics

Widespread consumption of narcotics has major impact on public health. The UNODC estimates that there are between 16 and 39m problem drug users, and approximately 200,000 drug-related deaths annually.[58] Rates of HIV infection, viral hepatitis, sexually transmitted diseases, and tuberculosis are also substantially higher among persons who use drugs illicitly.[59] Furthermore, research has indicated that multiple drug resistant tuberculosis is significantly higher among narcotics users than non-users,[60] and that using heroin may promote HIV drug resistance among HIV/AIDS patients.[61] Consequently, narcotics use not only exposes the population at large to a higher prevalence of contagious diseases, but also to more drug resistant strains of these diseases.

Counterfeits

Counterfeit goods can have serious public health implications. Unsafe foods, non-compliant electrical components, and faulty vehicle components are examples of this. But of all counterfeits, fake ineffective or substandard medicines likely pose the biggest threat.

Anti-malarial drugs constitute 25% of the total drug consumption in malaria-affected countries. Over 3bn people worldwide are at risk of catching the disease, which is endemic in over a hundred countries, mostly in the developing world. The most dangerous form of malaria parasite, *Plasmodium falciparum*, kills between 655,000 and 1.2m people every year, primarily in sub-Saharan Africa and South East Asia.[62]

Poor quality medication results in avoidable deaths and contributes to drug resistance. Falsified drugs are a major problem in this context. In 2012 the *Lancet*, a leading medical journal, published a review[63] of several studies to determine average rates of false anti-malarials. 36% of tested anti-malarials in seven South East Asian countries were classified as falsified, as were 20% in 21 sub-Saharan countries.[64]

Not only can low concentrations of active pharmaceutical ingredients in poor quality anti-malarials drugs provide inadequate protection, but can also contribute to the development of drug-resistant parasites. The authors of the Lancet article even went as far as arguing that that "production and distribution of counterfeit antimalarial drugs should be prosecuted as crimes against humanity."[65]

This problem is not limited to anti-malarials, with other studies and customs seizures indicating the enormous range of medicines that are affected by counterfeiting. Counterfeits frequently contain low quantities or no active ingredients, likely contributing to treatment failure. Falsified medication is a significant contributor to unnecessary and avoidable morbidity, mortality, drug resistance and loss of faith in the health care systems in low-income countries.[66] Despite the major challenge posed by fake and substandard drugs there is no global system for the mandatory reporting, assessment, and dissemination of information on suspicious medicines.[67]

Tobacco and Alcohol

Two categories of excise goods that are frequently associated with public health problems are tobacco and alcohol. Taxation of these products, other than raising government revenues, also serves to reduce consumption by making the products more expensive for consumers. The World Health Organisation (WHO)'s view on the illicit trade in tobacco is that it "increases the accessibility and affordability of tobacco products thus undermining tobacco control policies and severely burdening health systems" This in turn has a negative impact on public health and well-being, particularly of vulnerable groups such as the youth and the poor.[68] Furthermore, negative socio-economic implications can disproportionately be observed in developing regions and countries with economies in transition. The WHO identifies tobacco use as one of the most significant public health threats the world faces, killing nearly six million people per year. Considering that more than one in ten cigarettes smoked globally is estimated to be illegal, this is not an insignificant public health issue.

A 2008 paper in the British Medical Journal calculated that eliminating illicit tobacco could significantly reduce tobacco related deaths. The UK tobacco market was estimated to consist of 21% smuggled product, priced at half the legitimate price. An elasticity of demand at -0.72 (the rather high UK government estimate at the time) would result in a 0.72% decline in smoking per percentage increase in the tobacco price. The elimination of illicit tobacco would effectively double the price of 21% of the consumed products, resulting in a total decline in consumption of 7.2%. This would reduce the number of tobacco related deaths by at least 6,500 people per year, significantly higher than the 1,000 estimated annual UK deaths from smuggled illicit drugs.[69]

Alongside tobacco, the WHO considers alcohol to be "one of the world's leading health risks" and "a causal factor in more than 60 major types of diseases and injuries". It estimated the total number of deaths attributable to alcohol consumption to be 2.25 million in 2004—4% of all deaths worldwide and more than those caused by HIV/AIDS or tuberculosis.[70] Illicit alcohol sometimes grabs the headlines, such as in 2012 when 26 people were killed by methanol-contaminated counterfeit vodka and rum in the Czech Republic,[71] but like illicit tobacco the key public health problem is likely to be the prevalence of lower priced illicit products that drive up total consumption.

A 2012 Euromonitor study focusing on six Latin American countries estimated that 23% of the alcohol market was composed of illegal products and on average priced 30% below legitimate products.[72] In Europe, the WHO estimates that illicit alcohol is sold at roughly half the price of legitimate products.[73] A meta-study by James Fogarty calculated average price elasticities of demand for beer, wine and spirits at -0.44, -0.64 and -0.76 respectively,[74] suggesting that a significant prevalence of lower-priced illicit alcohol would increase total consumption.

Environmental Costs

The illegal trade in wildlife, illicit logging and illicit fishing contributes to the depletion of the stocks of these natural resources. The illegal trade in controlled chemicals (such as ozone-depleting substances) and the illegal disposal of hazardous waste have a negative impact on the environment. Critically, the damage caused to the ecosystem and the environmental stock damage eliminates future legitimate earnings on natural resources. In other words, if one takes into account the net present value of total economic losses in the future the total costs incurred far exceed the value of the illicit goods traded.[75]

In his paper *Global Scale and Impact of Illicit Trade* Justin Picard, co-founder of the non-governmental organisation (NGO) Black Market Watch, suggested the following approach to measuring the net present value of ecosystem losses due to illicit trade:

Step 1: Measure the value of ecosystem services
Step 2: Estimate rate of depletion of ecosystem resources
Step 3: Estimate proportion of ecosystem depletion due to illicit trade
Step 4: Use a discount factor per year for future losses on depleted ecosystems to calculate the net present value of total economic losses in the future[76]

Picard estimated an annual value of ecosystem services at US$115tr, a depletion rate of 0.13%, and that 10% of this depletion was due to illicit trade, resulting in US$14.95bn of ecosystem services that are permanently destroyed by illicit trade in the aforementioned categories. Using a discount factor of 3% per year for future losses, the net present value of the total economic losses in the future was estimated at US$489bn per year. This specific figure should not in any way be considered to be accurate. The critical point being that the true economic losses caused by environmental crime are manifold higher than the economic turnover due to the ecosystem destruction.

The illicit trade in many seemingly *normal* goods contribute to this irreversible damage. The primary goods themselves may have been improperly exploited, parts of manufactured products may have illicit sourcing, or toxic by-products of production processes may be illegally disposed of.

Additionally, other crimes not primarily seen as environmental crimes, such as the extensive problem of 'oil bunkering' in Nigeria, where oil is diverted from pipelines also have serious environmental impact. The oil theft results in significant oils spills and leaks that pollute water and soil, impacting human health, livelihoods, and food stocks.[77]

The Economic Costs of Illicit Trade

The aforementioned impacts of illicit trade, in terms of generating income for criminal non-state actors, government corruption, undermining border security, harming public health and environmental degradation are all associated with economic costs. But from an economic perspective the millions of drug users are not only a public health concern, but will also result in a cost to society through their reduced productivity and need for societal assistance, and a proportion will also engage in crime to finance their addiction further generating societal costs. Loss of human life can also be seen as an economic cost, with the elimination of future economic earnings of the victims.

The British Home Office report *Understanding organized crime: estimating the scale and the social and economic costs*[78] computed the total social and economic costs of organized crime (which also includes crimes other than illicit trade) to be £24bn, representing approximately 1% of British GDP. The report states that certain costs, such as costs of organized violence and homicide, violence associated with illicit drugs, and environmental crime related costs were not included due to the data challenges. Furthermore the report did not take into consideration costs incurred outside of British territory, such as global costs of intellectual property infringement to British rights holders. Nevertheless, in spite of these data gaps, the estimate provided in the report is a helpful indicator of the magnitude of the problem.

Some years earlier the U.S. Office of National Drug Control Policy (ONDCP) did estimate some of the narcotics related costs not captured in the UK study. It estimated that in 2002 the illicit drugs market generated societal costs totaling US$181bn due to healthcare costs (9%), productivity losses (71%) and other costs (20%). The single biggest cost—US$128bn in productivity losses—was the result of premature deaths, drug use–related illnesses, institutionalisation and hospitalisation, productivity losses of victims of crime, incarceration, and crime careers.[79] From ONDCP figures Justin Picard has extrapolated that every dollar spent on illicit narcotics generated indirect crime-related costs to society of US$1.54.[80]

The drugs sold in the United Stated have an economic impact beyond the nation's borders. The World Bank identifies the cocaine flow through Central America (estimated to represent 90% of U.S. supply) as the single most important factor behind the rising levels of violence in the region.[81] The Bank also argued that the direct economic costs of this violence as significant, possibly close to 8% of regional GDP if citizen security, law enforcement and health care are taken into account.[82] This is further exacerbated by the reductions in future growth potential "not just from the victims' lost wages and labour, but by polluting the investment climate and diverting scarce government resources to strengthen law enforcement rather than promote economic activity."[83]

The case of the economic consequences of illicit drug flows in Central America is an extreme example. But to some extent illicit flows of all types, all over the world, have negative impacts on the societies where they feed local crime groups. The diversion of state resources to combat the criminal entities controlling illicit trade can be particularly extreme in conflict situations. The rise of criminal networks controlling illicit trade forces governments to divert focus and resources to law enforcement efforts, at the expense of development.

Self-evidently, by displacing legitimate trade illicit trade reduces government tax revenue, an example of such costs is illustrated by a 2014 Global Financial Integrity study which found that over the previous decade, 25% of the value of all imports into the Philippines went unreported to customs officials.[84] Such extensive import under-invoicing is generally driven by a desire to reduce or eliminate the costs of customs duties and tariffs. Considering that taxes on international trade constituted 22% of total tax income in the Philippines, the fiscal impact is not negligible. Other studies suggest that trade mis-invoicing is a significant problem in the developing world as a whole.

Illicit exploitation, or theft, of natural mineral and hydrocarbon resources also constitutes a 'leakage' depriving states of export revenues. It is estimated that US$3–8 billion of Nigerian oil are stolen annually, and largely sold on the international market. Beyond the oil diversion itself, further costs were imposed on the nation: between 2007 and 2009, one government study found, attacks on oil infrastructure by Niger Delta militant groups shut down nearly half of Nigeria's onshore oilfields. These attacks slashed the country's oil exports, costing the state at least US$24bn in the first eight months of 2008 alone. Some 'warlords' are now receiving lucrative government contracts to guard the same infrastructure they previously attacked. From 2010 to 2012, the Nigerian National Petroleum Corporation spent US$2.3bn on pipeline security and repairs. Significant oil spills and leaks resulting from oil theft pollute water and soil also impact livelihoods and food stocks.[85]

Although the scale of the Nigerian oil theft is unparalleled, oil theft has been a source of revenue for militant groups in other parts of the world. In 2014 the Pentagon estimated that ISIS earned US$2 million per day on the sale of petroleum products (although airstrikes have likely reduced this source of revenue since).[86] The fact that non state actors (terrorists, insurgents or organized crime groups) accumulate revenues further diverts resources, as the government needs to combat economically empowered criminal entities.

Considering the multi-billion dollar scale of the illicit trade in counterfeit and excise goods it is no surprise that state's losses in tax revenues are substantial. But the total economic losses are much larger if the impact of intellectual property theft is taken fully into account. In 2013 the Commission on the theft of American Intellectual Property (IP Commission) estimated that that the annual losses for the American economy resulting from international intellectual property theft were comparable to the annual level of U.S. exports to Asia, i.e. over US$300bn. It also acknowledged that while the exact figure was hard to calculate, inadequacies in data or scope of government and private sector studies has led to o an underestimation of the problem. The Commission also seconded an assessment by the Commander of the United States Cyber Command and Director of the National Security Agency, General Keith Alexander, that the ongoing theft of IP was "the greatest transfer of wealth in history".[87] The IP Commission report further stated that enhanced intellectual property protection globally would add millions of jobs, boost research and development, investment and increase the growth of the American economy.[88]

The economic importance of enforcing intellectual property rights globally is also highlighted by the president of the European Patent Office who in 2014 stated:

> One in three jobs in the EU today is created in industrial sectors with an above average use of IP rights. These sectors account for almost 40% of the GDP and 90% of exports of the EU. They are a pillar of the competitiveness of the European economy at global level. Similarly, continued violation of these rights puts a serious threat to Europe's capacity to innovate and compete, and to lastingly secure economic growth and employment for its citizens. It is necessary, therefore, to improve and strengthen the use of IP rights not only in Europe, but also internationally.[89]

Synergistic Impact

Illicit trade does not operate in a vacuum, and there are synergies between different forms of illicit trade. Profits from one type of smuggling can empower a group involved in other contraband actives; the smuggling routes developed to bring in one good can be used for others; corrupted border officials that facilitate the passage of one type of good can be utilised to facilitate the passage of other items; and the demand for fraudulent documentation ensures the continued existence of such supply.

Even the mass-scale trade in relatively *harmless* products such as contraband consumer goods contributes to the necessary criminal infrastructure, which facilitates the smuggling of other lower volume but dangerous items such as firearms and explosives that can serve to empower criminals and terrorists. The Federal Bureau of Investigations (FBI) operation *Smoking Dragon* illustrated how an international smuggling ring that had started by bringing in contraband tobacco progressed to smuggling narcotics, counterfeit medicines and currency into the United States, and finally offered to smuggle in a variety of weapons including Chinese QW-2 surface-to-air missiles before being taken down by law enforcement.[90]

POLICY CONSIDERATIONS FOR ASSESSING ILLICIT TRADE

Illicit trade is a broad and varied collection of phenomena requiring a broad palette of coordinated policy responses, both at national and international levels. But unlike the threat of terrorism, which produces highly visible incidents, most of the times illicit trade remains below the surface, impeding the mobilisation of the prerequisite political will to address the threat. These challenges underline the need for better data to quantify and assess the impact of illicit trade, in order to empower policymakers to gauge their policy response more appropriately.

An intrinsic challenge is that it is virtually impossible to measure and put a value to certain negative effects of illicit trade, such as the corrosive effect on governance and the undermining of border security. Other impacts such as environmental and public health costs can in some cases be measured, as illustrated by the rough estimates of tobacco related deaths caused by contraband tobacco in the UK and Justin Picard's efforts to quantify net present value losses due ecosystem destruction caused by environmental crimes. The challenge here is twofold. The first—and fundamental—problem is that the underlying data upon which to base such estimates is frequently weak, or in many cases totally lacking (particularly in developing countries). Secondly, methodologies need to be developed, or fine-tuned, to produce such estimates. Looking at medicines as an example, it should be possible to develop a methodology to estimate (very roughly) the total number of deaths caused by falsified and substandard drugs provided that reliable data on the incidence of such drugs were the country is available.[91] Yet reliable data on the incidence does not exist as systematic and regular testing of major categories of drugs is not conducted in the countries where counterfeiting is most acute.

Calculating some of the direct economic impacts of illicit trade is theoretically more straightforward, but as the total cost estimate needs to factor in other indirect economic costs (such as the costs of crime generated, public health effects, environmental consequences, and other costs), which are dependent on other impact estimates gaining a comprehensive cost picture is very difficult. Additionally, in many areas the underlying data upon which to base even more straightforward economic cost impact estimates may be deeply flawed, or simply not exist. Consequently the foremost priority must be to obtain better data.

To name all the ways to obtain improved and more policy relevant data on illicit trade is not practical. The following three sub-sections will focus on three key areas of opportunity; two where data can significantly be improved, and one consideration that can ensure policy relevance of gathered data.

Developing Countries

If the rich world has reacted against narcotics, human trafficking and weapons because the impact at home is apparent—drug use, human exploitation and violence—then part of the solution to increase focus on other areas of illicit trade must lie in awakening 'enlightened self-interest'. In an increasingly interdependent world, where several of the developed world's trade partners are permeated by corruption and suffer from lack of effective enforcement capacity, a key part of the solution must lie not only in wealthier nations exporting enforcement capacity to developing countries, but also in supporting systematic efforts to map and quantify illicit trade. Otherwise assessing its impact will remain hampered, making an appropriate gauging of policy responses impossible.

Private Sector

Counterfeiting, which constitutes one of the largest categories of illicit trade, is an example of a key area where understanding is limited. The actors with the best insights are the affected companies, yet according to sources who have worked for the OECD and the World Economic Forum, corporations are very reluctant to share information about their counterfeiting challenges. Professor Tom Berglund at the Hanken School of Economics in Helsinki has stated that

> (...) to demand that companies should account more transparently about this is problematic. It goes against the companies' commercial interests to openly account for issues such as the prevalence of cheaper counterfeits which are difficult to differentiate from the original (...)" and "That makes it unreasonable to expect that companies shall become better at accounting for how they are affected by illicit trade. And this creates a larger societal responsibility, which ultimately means that the state must assume responsibility for deriving the foundation upon which it can evaluate how the national interests are affected by IP crimes.[92]

One possible solution—not advocated by Berglund—is that governments legislate to require corporations to account for the counterfeiting challenges they are facing. A further step could be to incentivise the corporations not only to report confirmed cases of counterfeiting (such as customs seizures where the trademark owner is alerted) but that they should estimate prevalence of counterfeiting in the markets where they operate and that they conduct business impact assessments taking estimated sales volume losses, trade mark damage, and other costs into consideration.

An alternative, or complementary, approach to direct government information requests, would be to encourage institutional investors to request more information concerning the business impact of counterfeiting and other forms of illicit trade from corporations.

There are a number of positive examples of private sector contributions enhancing understanding of illicit trade. For example, KPMG's *Project Sun*, which uses a systematic methodology based on collecting discarded cigarette packets, likely provides the most accurate estimates of the incidence of untaxed tobacco consumption in the European Union.[93] In India the Federation of Indian Chambers of Industry and Commerce commissioned a study attempting to quantify illicit markets in seven sectors, based on the difference arising between consumption expenditure and value of supply captured from sum of production from factories for domestic consumption, registered micro-enterprises and imports.[94] Encouraging commercial actors to conduct more studies shedding light on illicit trade could help fill important knowledge gaps.

National Interest

In an interdependent world the 'global big picture' serves an important role in contextualising the understanding of illicit trade, but individual states remain primarily driven by self-interest. States constitute the individual members of the international organisations, exercise authority over law enforcement agencies, and provide foreign assistance. Consequently little action will be taken against illicit trade, unless it is patently in the national interest of individual states to do so. Counterfeiting provides a clear example of the importance of generating data of relevance to the national interest.

The OECD's study, which sought to quantify the scale of counterfeiting as well as identifying some of the major flows, is an example of a study contributing to our understanding of the global nature of a problem. Irrespective of its strengths and shortcomings, the OECD study does not fully identify which states are the losers from the illicit trade it sought to quantify, as IP owners may be based in one jurisdiction, production in a second, and the customer in a third. Here the simple approach adopted by the Japan Patent Office, conducting an annual survey on losses suffered by Japanese companies due to counterfeiting, provides an example of data more relevant to the national interest in addressing illicit trade.[95] Furthermore, the Japanese coordinated policy structure, with intellectual property strategy set and coordinated by the Prime Minister's Office, also facilitates comprehensive approach to intellectual property enforcement. As it so happens Japan is a major supporter of the World Intellectual Property Organization (WIPO), WCO, as well as bilateral efforts to enhance customs capacity building in other countries, and it was a major proponent of the Anti-Counterfeiting Trade Agreement (ACTA).

By contrast the EU is a political union of 28 member states that lacks Japan's high level policy coordination regarding IP strategy, and has so far not published studies that capture what proportion of IP intense European businesses is affected by global counterfeiting. Perhaps unsurprisingly, despite the centrality of intellectual property to European exports, the EU has not been as robust as Japan in its approach to promoting and exporting global intellectual property rights enforcement.[96] Relevant data, coupled with a more coordinated policy approach, could change that.

THE BIG PICTURE

If the primary interest in acquiring better data on illicit trade is to inform policy makers, then one also needs to consider how the contextualisation of that information can enhance its impact. In fact, data on individual forms of illicit trade may have additional value in a broader illicit trade perspective. First, inherent synergies among different forms of illicit trade make a given set of data of relevance to a broader array of stakeholders. Second, some of the solutions to address illicit trade, such as enhancing border security, impact multiple categories of illicit trade. Third, it is easier to mobilise political will around one mega-problem rather than several smaller separate issues. In this context, it is vital to highlight that the response to the illicit trade mega-problem requires engagement from a broader range of actors than law enforcement agencies alone, and therefore illicit trade ought to be mainstreamed and integrated into the policy agendas of development, security, and trade actors.

NOTES

1. 'OECD Task Force on Countering Illicit Trade (TF-CIT)', *Organisation for Economic Co-operation and Development (OECD)*, http://www.oecd.org/gov/risk/oecdtaskforceoncounteringillicittrade.htm.
2. Klaus Von Lampe, *Definitions of Organized Crime*, 5 January 2017, http://www.organized-crime.de/organizedcrimedefinitions.htm.
3. 'Illicit Trade Report 2012', *World Customs Organisation*, 2013, p. 2, http://www.wcoomd.org/en/topics/key-issues/~/~/media/WCO/Public/Global/PDF/Topics/Enforcement%20and%20Compliance/Activities%20and%20Programmes/Illicit%20Trade%20Report%202012/WCO%20REPORT%202013%20-%20BR.ashx.
4. 'New UN campaign highlights financial and social costs of transnational organized crime', *UN News Centre*, 16 July 2012, http://www.un.org/apps/news/story.asp?NewsID=42480#.VLAO8ivF-So.
5. 'Illegal Trade in Environmentally Sensitive Goods: Executive Summary', Paris: *OECD*, October 2012, http://www.oecd.org/tad/envtrade/ExecutiveSummaryIllegalTradeEnvSensitiveGoods.pdf.
6. Luk Joossens, David Merriman, Hana Ross et al, 'The impact of eliminating the global illicit cigarette trade', *Addiction*, vol. 105, no. 9, September 2010, pp. 1640–1649.
7. 'Global Status Report on Alcohol and Health 2014', *World Health Organization (WHO)* (Luxembourg: World Health Organization, 2014), http://www.who.int/substance_abuse/publications/global_alcohol_report/msb_gsr_2014_1.pdf?ua=1.
8. OECD, *Trade in Counterfeit and Pitated Goods: Mapping the Economic Impact* (Paris, OECD Publishing, 2016).
9. 'JPO Compiles FY 2015 Survey Report on Losses Caused by Counterfeiting', *Ministry of Economy, Trade and Industry*, 10 March 2016, http://www.meti.go.jp/english/press/2016/0310_01.html.
10. 'Thousands of tonnes of fake food and drink seized in INTERPOL-Europe operation', *INTERPOL*, 14 February 2014, http://www.interpol.int/News-and-media/News/2014/N2014-022.
11. 'INTERPOL operation nets fakes worth USD 50 million across Asia', *INTERPOL*, 22 September 2014, http://www.interpol.int/News-and-media/News/2014/N2014-179.
12. 'Operation Biyela: Record Seizure of Illicit Medicines in Africa', *International Institute of Research against Counterfeit Medicines*, June 2013, http://www.iracm.com/en/2013/06/operation-biyela-record-seizure-of-illicit-medicines-in-africa/.

13. 'Transnational Organized Crime: The Globalized Illegal Economy', *United Nations Office on Drugs and Crime (UNODC)*, August 2012, http://www.unodc.org/documents/toc/factsheets/TOC12_fs_general_EN_HIRES.pdf.
14. 'Crime in the Age of Technology—Europol's Serious and Organized Crime Threat Assessment 2017'.
15. Europol, *The European Union Serious and Organized Crime Threat Assessment 2017* (The Hague, European Police Office 2017).
16. 'Trafficking in illicit goods and counterfeiting', *INTERPOL*, http://www.interpol.int/Crime-areas/Trafficking-in-illicit-goods-and-counterfeiting/Trafficking-in-illicit-goods-and-counterfeiting.
17. John Otis, 'The FARC and Colombia's Illegal Drug Trade', *Wilson Center*, November 2014, http://www.wilsoncenter.org/sites/default/files/Otis_FARCDrugTrade2014.pdf.
18. 'The Global Afghan Opium Trade: A Threat Assessment', Vienna: *UNODC*, July 2011, http://www.unodc.org/documents/data-and-analysis/Studies/Global_Afghan_Opium_Trade_2011-web.pdf.
19. 'Profile: Mokhtar Belmokhtar', *BBC News*, 15 June 2015, http://www.bbc.com/news/world-africa-21061480.
20. Jonathan Masters and Mohammed Aly Sergie, 'Al-Shabab', *Council on Foreign Relations (CFR) – Backgrounders*, 13 March 2015, http://www.cfr.org/somalia/al-shabab/p18650.
21. Karl Lallerstedt, 'Syria and Sweden: A distant conflict with serious consequences at home', *Frivärld: Stockholm Free World Forum*, 6 February 2015, http://www.frivarld.se/rapporter/syria-sweden/.
22. James D. Fearon, 'Why Do Some Civil Wars Last So Much Longer Than Others?', *Journal of Peace Research*, vol. 41, no. 3, 2004, pp. 275–301, http://www.saramitchell.org/fearon.pdf.
23. Moisés Naím, 'Mafia States: Organized Crime Takes Office', *Foreign Affairs*, May/June 2012 Issue, http://www.foreignaffairs.com/articles/137529/moises-naim/mafia-states.
24. Santiago Villaveces-Izquierdo and Catalina Uribe Burcher, 'Illicit Networks and Politics in the Baltic States', *International Institute for Democracy and Electoral Assistance (International IDEA)* (Stockholm: International IDEA 2013), http://www.idea.int/publications/illicit-networks-and-politics/loader.cfm?csModule=security/getfile&pageid=60609.
25. Ibid.
26. James Bargent, 'Colombia Criminals Use Paraguay Contraband Cigarettes to Launder Drug Money', *InSight Crime*, 24 March 2014, http://www.insightcrime.org/news-briefs/colombia-criminals-use-paraguay-contraband-cigarettes-to-launder-drug-money.

27. Paul Rexton Kan, Bruce E. Bechtol, Jr. and Robert M. Collins, 'Criminal Sovereignty: Understanding North Korea's Illicit International Activities', *Strategic Studies Institute*, March 2010, http://www.strategicstudiesinstitute.army.mil/pdffiles/pub975.pdf.

28. Vadzim Smok, 'The art of smuggling in Belarus', *Open Democracy*, 2 February 2015, https://www.opendemocracy.net/od-russia/vadzim-smok/art-of-smuggling-in-belarus.

29. Malcolm Rees, 'Mugabe link to illegal cigarette trade', *Times Live*, 29 December 2013, http://www.timeslive.co.za/africa/2013/12/29/mugabe-link-to-illegal-cigarette-trade1.

30. Malcolm Rees, 'Edward Zuma in tobacco feud', *Moneyweb*, 25 September 2013, http://www.moneyweb.co.za/archive/edward-zuma-in-tobacco-feud/.

31. 'Guinea-Bissau ex-navy chief in drugs arrest', *BBC News*, 5 April 2013, http://www.bbc.com/news/world-africa-22030847.

32. Michael Miklaucic and Moisés Naím, 'The Criminal State', in Michael Miklaucic and Jacqueline Brewer (eds.), *Convergence: Illicit Networks and National Security in the Age of Globalization* (Washington DC: National Defence University Press, 2013), pp. 149–170.

33. James Risen, 'Reports Link Karzai's Brother to Afghanistan Heroin Trade', *The New York Times*, 4 October 2008, http://www.nytimes.com/2008/10/05/world/asia/05afghan.html?pagewanted=all&_r=0.

34. Discussions and interviews with the author.

35. Guy Dinmore, 'Berlusconi ally extradited to Italy from Lebanon', *Financial Times*, 13 June 2014, http://www.ft.com/intl/cms/s/0/ea4bbf6e-f2eb-11e3-85cd-00144feabdc0.html#axzz3UN5C2lXW.

36. Michael Day, 'Silvio Berlusconi's links with Italian organized crime confirmed', *The Independent*, 12 May 2014, http://www.independent.co.uk/news/world/europe/silvio-and-the-cosa-nostra-berlusconis-links-with-italian-organized-crime-confirmed-9358790.html. The dominant political figure in post war Italy, seven-time Prime Minister Giulio Andreotti, was put on trial for mafia association. In July 2003 the appeal court of Palermo acquitted him on charges of complicity with the mafia, but it upheld the prosecution's case that the former prime minister had been engaged in criminal association until 1980. The charges lapsed under the statute of limitations. These two court rulings confirm long running collusion between the mafia and the most powerful politicians in Italy. See Guy Dinmore, 'Former Italian PM Giulio Andreotti dies' *Financial Times*, 6 May 2013, http://www.ft.com/cms/s/0/949e39b0-b643-11e2-b1e5-00144feabdc0.html#ixzz3UOSwwPOC.

37. Jane Croft, 'Putin Accused of presiding over 'mafia state' at Litvinenko probe', *Financial Times*, 27 January 2015, http://www.ft.com/intl/cms/s/0/998d690c-a62c-11e4-9bd3-00144feab7de.html#axzz3UuujrUQt.

38. Mark Galeotti, 'How the Invasion of Ukraine is Shaking Up the Global Crime Scene,' *Vice*, 6 November 2014, http://www.vice.com/read/how-the-invasion-of-ukraine-is-shaking-up-the-global-crime-scene-1106.

39. Ivan Briscoe, Catalina Perdomo, and Catalina Uribe Burcher (eds.), 'Illicit Networks and Politics in Latin America', *International IDEA*, 2014, http://www.idea.int/publications/illicit-networks-and-politics-in-latin-america/en.cfm.

40. Ibid.

41. Ibid.

42. 'Anti-Corruption Measures in EU Border Control', *Sofia, BG: Center for the Study of Democracy* (Frontex 2012), http://www.csd.bg/artShow.php?id=16109.

43. Ibid.

44. Martin Santa, 'Slovaks find railway smuggling tunnel to Ukraine', *Reuters*, 19 July 2012, http://www.reuters.com/article/2012/07/19/us-slovakia-ukraine-tunnel-idUSBRE86I0ZO20120719.

45. 'Inside Mexico's Drug Tunnels', *TIME*, http://content.time.com/time/photogallery/0,29307,1895418,00.html.

46. Harriet Sherwood, 'Inside the tunnels Hamas built: Israel's struggle against new tactic in Gaza war', *The Guardian*, 2 August 2014, http://www.theguardian.com/world/2014/aug/02/tunnels-hamas-israel-struggle-gaza-war.

47. Sean Gallagher, 'Update: Russians capture cigarette-smuggling drone', *Ars Technica*, 16 May 2014, http://arstechnica.com/tech-policy/2014/05/russians-capture-cigarette-smuggling-drone/.

48. Nick Valencia and Michael Martinez, 'Drone carrying drugs crashes south of U.S. border', *CNN*, 23 January 2015, http://edition.cnn.com/2015/01/22/world/drug-drone-crashes-us-mexico-border/.

49. 'Drug submarine seized by Colombian navy', 15 February 2011, http://www.bbc.co.uk/news/world-latin-america-12461089.

50. Henry Samuel, "Narco-torpedoes' and frogmen: drug smuggling ring busted in Rotterdam," *The Telegraph*, 26 April 2013, http://www.telegraph.co.uk/news/worldnews/europe/netherlands/10021140/Narco-torpedoes-and-frogmen-drug-smuggling-ring-busted-in-Rotterdam.html.

51. 'Iran President Rouhani hits out at US sanctions', *BBC News*, 30 August 2014, http://www.bbc.com/news/world-middle-east-28997452.

52. 'The Distribution of Iranian Ammunition in Africa: Evidence from a nine-country investigation', *Conflict Armament Research* (London: Conflict Armament Research LTD, 2012), http://www.conflictarm.com/wp-content/uploads/2014/09/Iranian_Ammunition_Distribution_in_Africa.pdf.

53. Karl Lallerstedt and Mikael Wigell, 'Illicit Trade Flows: How to deal with the neglected economic and security threat', *Finnish Institute of International Affairs (FIIA)*, Briefing Paper 151, 12 March 2014, http://www.fiia.fi/en/publication/405/illicit_trade_flows/.

54. Kan, Bechtol, Jr. and Collins, 'Criminal Sovereignty: Understanding North Korea's Illicit International Activities'.

55. Ibid.

56. 'Record number of over 1.2 million first time asylum seekers registered in 2015', *Eurostat News Release*, 44/2016, 4 March 2016, http://ec.europa.eu/eurostat/documents/2995521/7203832/3-04032016-AP-EN.pdf/.

57. Mike Giglio and Munzer al-Awad, 'ISIS Operative: This Is How We Send Jihadis to Europe,' *Buzzfeed News*, 30 January 2015, http://www.buzzfeed.com/mikegiglio/isis-operative-this-is-how-we-send-jihadis-to-europe#.cp0od4dZyE.

58. 'Global drug use stable, but nearly 200,000 drug-related deaths still recorded—UN report', 26 June 2014. http://www.un.org/apps/news/story.asp?NewsID=48138#.VKkSDcYtx1M.

59. 'Integrated Prevention Services for HIV Infection, Viral Hepatitis, Sexually Transmitted Diseases, and Tuberculosis for Persons Who Use Drugs Illicitly: Summary Guidance from CDC and the U.S. Department of Health and Human Services', *Centers for Disease Control and Prevention*, Recommendations and Reports 9 November 2012 / 61(RR05), pp. 1–40, http://www.cdc.gov/mmwr/preview/mmwrhtml/rr6105a1.htm.

60. M Ruddy, Y Balabanova, C Graham, I Fedorin, N Malomanova, E Elisarova, S Kuznetznov, G Gusarova, S Zakharova, A Melentyev, E Krukova, V Golishevskaya, V Erokhin, I Dorozhkova and F Drobniewski, 'Rates of drug resistance and risk factor analysis in civilian and prison patients with tuberculosis in Samara Region, Russia', *Thorax,* vol. 60, no. 2, 2005, pp. 130–135.

61. B Liang, X Yang, J Jiang, B Zhou, H Chen, R Chen, F Zhao, P Pan, J Huang, L Ye and H Liang, 'The efficacy of antiviral therapy and drug resistance analysis among HIV/AIDS patients with heroin addiction in Guangxi Zhuang Autonomous Region,' *Zhonghua Yu Fang Yi Xue Za Zhi,* vol. 48, no. 10, October 2014, pp. 851–856, http://www.ncbi.nlm.nih.gov/pubmed/25573121.

62. Gaurvika ML Nayyar, Joel G. Bremen, Paul N. Newton and James Herrington, 'Poor-quality antimalarial drugs in southeast Asia and sub-Saharan Africa', *The Lancet*, vol. 12, no. 6, June 2012, pp. 488–496, http://www.thelancet.com/journals/lancetid/article/PIIS1473-3099(12)70064-6/abstract.

63. Ibid.

64. In sub-Saharan Africa 35% of all tested drugs failed chemical analysis, suggesting that substandard medication is a broader problem beyond counterfeiting. In the Asian countries 35% failed chemical analysis, a very similar proportion to that classified as falsified. Ibid.

65. Ibid.

66. Ibid.

67. Paul N Newton, Patricia Tabernero, Prabha Dwivedi, Maria J Culzoni, Maria Eugenia Mange, Isabel Swarnidoss, Dallas Mildenhall, Michael D Green, Richard Jähnke, Miguel dos Santos de Oliveira, Julia Simao, Nicholas J White and Facundo M Fernandez, 'Falsified medicines in Africa: all talk, no action,' *The Lancet*, vol. 2, September 2014, e509–510, http://www.thelancet.com/pdfs/journals/langlo/PIIS2214-109X(14)70279-7.pdf.

68. 'Protocol to Eliminate Illicit Trade in Tobacco Products opened for signature', *WHO*, 10 January 2013, http://www.who.int/mediacentre/news/releases/2013/fctc_20130110/en/.

69. Robert West, Joy Townsend, Luk Joossens, Deborah Arnott and Sarah Lewis, 'Why combatting tobacco smuggling is a priority', *British Medical Journal*, 337:a1933, October 2008, http://www.bmj.com/content/337/bmj.a1933.

70. 'Global Status Report on Alcohol and Health', *WHO* (Geneva: WHO, 2011), http://www.who.int/substance_abuse/publications/global_alcohol_report/msbgsruprofiles.pdf.

71. Rebecca Smithers, 'New year revellers warned of dangers of counterfeit alcohol', *The Guardian*, 31 December 2012, http://www.theguardian.com/society/2012/dec/31/new-year-fake-alcohol-warning.

72. 'The Illegal Alcoholic Beverages Market in Six Countries', *Euromonitor International*, 2013, http://www.euromonitor.com/medialibrary/PDF/ILLEGALALCOHOLEUROMONITOR.pdf.

73. Dirk W Lachenmeier, *Unrecorded and illicit alcohol*, http://www.euro.who.int/__data/assets/pdf_file/0020/191360/2-Unrecorded-and-illicit-alcohol.pdf.

74. James Fogarty, 'The Demand for Beer, Wine and Spirits: Insights from a Meta Analysis Approach', *American Association of Wine Economists*, Working Paper no. 31, November 2008, http://www.wine-economics.org/workingpapers/AAWE_WP31.pdf.

75. Justin Picard, 'Can We Estimate the Global Scale and Impact of Illicit Trade?', in Miklaucic and Brewer (eds.), *Convergence: Illicit Networks and National Security in the Age of Globalization*, pp. 37–60.

76. Ibid.

77. Christina Katsouris and Aaron Sayne, 'Nigeria's Criminal Crude: International Options to Combat the Export of Stolen Oil', *Chatham House*, September 2013, http://www.chathamhouse.org/sites/files/chathamhouse/public/Research/Africa/0913pr_nigeriaoil.pdf.

78. Hannah Mills, Sara Skodbo and Peter Blyth, 'Understanding Organized Crime: estimating the scale and the social and economic costs', *UK Home Office*, Research Report 73, October 2013, https://www.gov.uk/government/uploads/system/uploads/attachment_data/file/246390/horr73.pdf.

79. 'The Economic Costs of Drug Abuse in the United States, 1992–2002', *Executive Office of the President* (Washington DC: Office of National Drug Control Policy, December 2004), https://www.ncjrs.gov/ondcppubs/publications/pdf/economic_costs.pdf.

80. Picard, 'Can We Estimate the Global Scale and Impact of Illicit Trade?', in Miklaucic and Brewer (eds.), *Convergence: Illicit Networks and National Security in the Age of Globalization*.

81. 'Crime and Violence in Central America: A Development Challenge', *The World Bank*, 2011, http://siteresources.worldbank.org/INTLAC/Resources/FINAL_VOLUME_I_ENGLISH_CrimeAndViolence.pdf.

82. Ibid., p. ii.

83. Ibid.

84. Dev Kar and Brian LeBlanc, 'Illicit Financial Flows to and from the Philippines: A Study in Dynamic Simulation, 1960–2011', *Global Financial Integrity*, February 2014, http://www.gfintegrity.org/wp-content/uploads/2014/05/Illicit-Financial-Flows-to-and-from-the-Philippines-Final-Report.pdf.

85. Katsouris and Sayne, 'Nigeria's Criminal Crude: International Options to Combat the Export of Stolen Oil'.

86. Keith Johnson, 'U.S. Strikes ISIS Oil Installations', *Foreign Policy*, 24 September 2014, http://foreignpolicy.com/2014/09/24/u-s-strikes-isis-oil-installations/.

87. 'The Report of the Commission on the Theft of American Intellectual Property', *The IP Commission Report*, May 2013, p.2, http://www.ipcommission.org/report/IP_Commission_Report_052213.pdf.

88. Ibid. A 2017 update to the IP Commission report estimated that the annual cost to the U.S. economy continued to exceed US$ 225 billion in counterfeit goods, pirated software and the theft of trade secrets, and could be as high as US$ 600 billion. 'Update to the IP Commission

Report', *The Theft of American Intellectual Property: Reassessments of the Challenge and United States Policy*, 2017, http://www.ipcommission. org/report/IP_Commission_Report_Update_2017.pdf.

89. *Illicit Trade Flows: How to deal with the neglected economic and security threat*, Finnish Institute of International Affairs Briefing Paper No. 151 (Helsinki: Finnish Institute of International Affairs: March 12, 2014).

90. 'Operation Smoking Dragon', *Federal Bureau of Investigation (FBI)*, 5 July 2011, http://www.fbi.gov/news/stories/2011/july/dragon_070511.

91. Some such efforts have been made despite the data challenges. An organisation called the International Policy Network released a report in 2009 estimating that counterfeit antimalarial and tuberculosis medication alone caused 700,000 death per year, but the reliability of this figure is highly questionable. In 2013 the UN publication Africa Renewal cited a WHO estimate that 100,000 people died every year from counterfeit drugs in Africa, but the methodology used to derive this estimate is not clear. See Jocelyne Sambira, 'Counterfeit drugs raise Africa's temperature', *Africa Renewal*, May 2013, http://www.un.org/africarenewal/magazine/may-2013/counterfeit-drugs-raise-africa's-temperature.

92. Karl Lallerstedt and Patrick Krassén, 'How leading companies are affected by counterfeiting and IP infringement—A study of the NASDAQ OMX 30 Stockholm Index', *The Swedish Confederation of Enterprise (Svenskt Näringsliv)*, May 2015, http://www.svensktnaringsliv.se/migration_catalog/Rapporter_och_opinionsmaterial/Rapporter/omx30_english_webb-pdf_617515.html/BINARY/OMX30_English_webb.pdf.

93. 'Project Sun: A study of the illicit cigarette market in the European Union 2013 Results', *KPMG*, 2014 http://www.pmi.com/eng/media_center/media_kit/documents/sun%20report%202013.pdf.

94. 'Socio-Economic Impact of Counterfeiting, Smuggling and Tax Evasion in Seven Key Indian Industry Sectors', *Federation of Indian Chambers of Commerce and Industry*, 2012, http://www.ficci.com/publication-page. asp?spid=20190.

95. 'FY2013 Survey Report on Losses Caused by Counterfeiting Was Compiled'.

96. The fact that the EU is a political union of 28 member states is also a factor that makes coordinated policy prioritisation challenging, but that does not remove the need for underlying data indicating the loss suffered to EU business by global counterfeiting.

CHAPTER 5

Catalysing and Evaluating Development Responses to Organized Crime

Tuesday Reitano

Abstract The author points to some of the practical implications for the way development initiatives should be considered in response to transnational organized crime, including the means by which they should be measured, as part of a shift towards a more integrated approach.

The chapter shows, while it has been conclusively proven that security or justice led strategies will not be successful on their own; the more recent evidence is that development led strategies are similarly unlikely to be unilaterally successful. They are, however, fundamental to a long-term and sustainable solution to some of the most compelling global manifestations of organized crime challenges, to mitigating their impact on the world's most vulnerable and building resilience of individuals and communities to resist their influence in the future.

Keywords Crime • Development • Corruption • Integrated approach

Building on the preceding discussion, the aim of the following pages is to point to some of the practical implications for the way development initiatives should be considered in response to transnational organized

T. Reitano (✉)
Global Initiative against Transnational Organized Crime, Geneva, Switzerland

© The Author(s) 2018   111
V. Comolli (ed.), *Organized Crime and Illicit Trade*,
https://doi.org/10.1007/978-3-319-72968-8_5

crime, including the means by which they should be measured, as part of a shift towards a more integrated approach.

If the previous chapters have demonstrated anything, it is that the challenge presented by organized crime is diverse, and its impact on development across all of its sectors is considerable, damaging and difficult to reverse. A consistent theme of the sectoral narrative has been that while we are perhaps becoming more able to identify the harms of organized crime on development, and in some notable cases there is a significant body of concerned rhetoric within the international community, responses have been more of a challenge.

The classic conceptualisation of organized crime as a law enforcement and criminal justice issue has led to security-first strategies focused around border control and policing, and these have largely failed to deliver results. Reconceptualising this within a development framework as part of an integrated approach has garnered policy attention, but there is little genuine understanding of what that means in practice.[1]

The emphasis on the need for *integrated* approaches, as opposed to security-led, or development-led, or fragmented initiatives that do not form a cohesive and mutually reinforcing package of interventions, is important. As the discussion in the subsequent session will show, while it has been conclusively proven that security or justice led strategies will not be successful on their own; the more recent evidence is that development led strategies are similarly unlikely to be unilaterally successful. They are, however, fundamental to a long-term and sustainable solution to some of the most compelling global manifestations of organized crime challenges, to mitigating their impact on the world's most vulnerable and building resilience of individuals and communities to resist their influence in the future.

In part this is because organized crime itself, and the concepts that are used around it, mean different things to different people. There is no single and accepted definition of organized crime, and thus when seeking multi-lateral or multi-sectoral action a common understanding can prove even more elusive. The issue of transnational organized crime, because it touches upon the portfolios of so many different stakeholders, is actually precisely the sort of topic to bring multiple strands of government together, but key tensions reinforce the traditional divide between security and development narratives: conceptual, causal, institutional, and motivational. These tensions affect the lens through which the challenge is looked at, who is charged with leading interventions, where funding is found and the means of delivery.[2]

It is clear that development community lacks a framework around which to understand, analyse and respond to organized crime.[3] However, this is a situation that needs urgent resolution as the inclusion of organized crime within the Sustainable Development Goals (SDGs) provides development actors with a clear mandate to act whereas previously this mandate had been less explicit. Furthermore, at the international level, the development finance structures have not previously facilitated integrated approaches, as the categorisation of what could be considered official development assistance (ODA) did not necessarily match the reality of many contexts where varied support to fight organized crime was needed. This complication has been rectified as part of *Financing for Development* effort to modernise ODA processes currently underway, with a new measure of "total official support for development" (TOSD) to capture more aspects of security and justice spending.[4]

With both mandate and financing issues moving the requirement to respond to organized crime more clearly into the development space, the subsequent section of this chapter seeks to explore how such a response might be catalysed, what such a response might look like, and how its success might be measured.

RETHINKING THE MEASUREMENT OF ORGANIZED CRIME

One challenge, which is particularly pertinent as questions around measuring progress against the SDGs are considered, is what the marker of a *successful* response to organized crime is. This is important, as the way that success is measured tends to drive the toolbox of approaches that are brought to the table in response.

Typically, studies of the scope and scale of organized crime measure the size of the flow, which in turn is extrapolated on the basis of seizures of the contraband. With seizures as the primary metric of success, this had led to an over-emphasis on interdiction and disruption strategies, rather than genuine investigations into the networks perpetrating those flows. Furthermore, the utility of the indicator itself is reducing as corruption and state complicity in criminal markets orients around protecting the trade rather than prosecuting it. The impact corruption has on seizure data can clearly be seen in the case of Guinea-Bissau: in 2012 the World Drug Report speculated the West African route had decreased in importance because there were no major drug seizures since 2008. However, those working in the region could see visible evidence of an increase in drug flows.[5] Seizure rates have proven to be a better measure of the effectiveness of government and law enforcement rather than an indication of the scale of organized crime itself, and speak nothing about the impact that it is having on the security and development of the communities along a route.[6]

With the discussions around the establishment of the SDG framework and subsequent indicators to measure progress, an alternative marker of using 'illicit financial flows' (IFFs) as a proxy measure of organized crime has come forward. Goal 16 of the SDGs contains the governance and rule of law principles that were absent in the Millenium Development Goals (MDG) framework, and with such largely nebulous and qualitative concepts at play such as quality of governance and justice, the ability to find suitable quantifiable indicators of success has proven a subject of significant debate. Within this agenda, the direct reference to organized crime is found in Goal 16.4, "By 2030, significantly reduce illicit financial and arms flows, strengthen the recovery and return of stolen assets and combat all forms of organized crime".[7] For Goal 16.4, which aggregates a number of diverse concepts under one unwieldy chapeau, on the list formally approved by the UN, the indicators for 16.4 relate only to reducing IFFs and the proportion of seized small arms.[8]

Ground-breaking work by Global Financial Integrity (GFI) has created widespread acceptance of the use of the International Monetary Fund (IMF) balance of payments and residual trade statistics as an acceptable measure for IFFs, and thus for organized crime as a whole.[9] Yet GFI's work that focuses on the reporting of licit trade, therefore by definition excludes the actual volume of criminal activity that occurs outside of the legitimate economy—activities like drug trafficking, the wildlife trade or human trafficking—which are precisely what we would seek in a response to organized crime. Furthermore, whilst GFI's metric focuses on volume, it does not speak to the impact of such flows and therefore provides little assistance to policymakers and practitioners who are seeking to understand the implications for development response and prioritise their assistance.

The impact of illicit outflows is compounded when the opportunity cost to development is considered. Money transferred out of domestic economies does not benefit from the multiplier effects of domestic use on economic growth and job creation. The argument often made is that trade diverted, and the legitimate tax revenue lost, undermine the capacity for governments to invest in social service delivery and development. For example, it has been estimated that the African economy would have expanded by more than 60% if even the most conservative estimate of IFFs had been invested in the domestic economy, and gross domestic product (GDP) per capita could have been 15% higher.[10] The *World Development Report 2011* observed that firms in sub-Saharan Africa lost a higher percentage of sales to illicit trade and crime, and spend a higher percentage of sales on security than any other region.[11]

But this is not only an issue about money, and this is the risk of allowing IFFs to become the next dominant metric around which organized crime responses are measured. While Africa may not be the region with the greatest absolute levels of IFFs, it is arguably the region where the negative impacts of illicit flows are most acutely felt. The ability to divert resources and commit illegal acts thrives in contexts where the capacity of state institutions is weak and regulatory capacity is low. Illicit activity also undermines the integrity of institutions through corruption, which, in certain states over time has undermined the rule of law, damaged the relationship between citizens and the state and created situations of impunity. Perception surveys across the continent undertaken by the civil society initiative Afrobarometer, indicate widespread levels of citizen disenfranchisement, a 'democracy deficit' where leaders are seen to be failing to deliver results on the democratic process, and extensive corruption, most namely in the police and security sector.[12] Corruption has been widely shown to be the greatest burden for the poorest in society, with the most significant impact on their ability to achieve sustainable livelihood, social justice and other basic development goals.

A focus on trade and mispricing might identify some aspects of the weakness of state institutions to regulate trade, but it will not capture the broader framework of state erosion or impunity and the broader development. Furthermore, as the responses to this agenda have already shown, the 2015 report of the *High Level Panel on Illicit Financial Flows from Africa* being one example, the types of initiatives to counter an IFF-centric view of organized crime have been embedded in discussions around tax policy and regulation, and have placed the onus on foreign corporations to achieve higher standards of business ethics.[13] While important, these are measures that will have little impact on the 60% or more of the underserved and vulnerable populations operating in the global shadow economy; nor do they address the grand corruption that systematically perpetuate and protect such flows.

In seeking a more responsive and multi-dimensional set of metrics, therefore, it is clear that one single indicator is unlikely to fit the bill. Arguably there is a need for a basket of indicators that will provide data across two categories, the scale of organized crime and its impact. Measurements of scale would analyse the depth and forms that organized crime has assumed, and measurements of impact would look at the ways that organized crime is engaging with communities, states and the natural environment. It is worth noting that the juxtaposition between scale and impact as the two outputs do not necessarily rise and fall with each other. In fact, a decrease in the scale of organized crime can result in a greater impact on communities. For example, in Honduras, a decrease in cocaine trafficking resulted in greater competition between criminal actors and higher levels of violence and homicide.[14]

Criminal justice data remains important, but it needs to widen beyond seizures towards a nuanced combination of crime data, seizure data, law enforcement indictments on typical organized crimes, as well as homicides and other forms of crime. Not only serious crimes have value: kidnappings, disappearances, unexplained arsons, and sharp changes in crime trends may be important indicators in changing crime types when local contexts are taken into account. Unsolved homicides often also have value, as homicides can typically be divided in to emotional attacks on intimates and cold-blooded killings executed by organized criminal groups. The perpetrators of the first type of homicide are usually arrested, while the perpetrators of the second category are not and the homicides go unsolved.[15]

A critical element of moving towards people-centric and human security focused responses will be the greater use of public perceptions data. In the first place, public perceptions of the presence of organized is essential to supplement and interpret criminal data, as there is a tendency for organized crime actions to go unreported, particularly in environments where corruption is a concern. Surveys, such as the International Crime Victims Survey, which measures crimes that affect ordinary citizens on a large scale, found that the less confidence individuals had in the police the less likely they were to report *conventional* or not as serious crimes. Thus, in regions such as Latin America and Africa—where observers are witnessing high levels of organized crime—there are very low crime reporting rates.[16]

Perhaps more important, however, is the value of public perceptions data in measuring and understanding the impact of organized crime. This is arguably the most challenging and complex category to measure, as it focuses more on the intangible effects of organized crime in areas such as on increased levels of insecurity and diminishing public service delivery. Surveys on public perceptions of safety can reflect increased levels of violence and fear in communities as a result of organized crime, while surveys of local businesses can uncover extortion rates and reflect the impact organized is having on local economies. At the same time they may also reveal the level of dependency and concern that illicit markets and actors present for the community, which can in turn nuance the direction of international investment. For example, despite great concern by the international community regarding the growth of illicit trafficking in the Sahel, a 2014 public perceptions survey undertaken by the Danish Demining Group found that community members ranked insecurity almost bottom in their list of priorities, far below other more pressing developmental and livelihood concerns such as food availability, poverty and access to water.[17] There are number of sources already available and systematically collected that could contribute to such a composite public perceptions indicator, including the Ease of and Cost of doing business surveys compiled annually by the World Bank. Gallup Analytics collects global data on issues such as confidence in leadership, confidence in the military and the police, corruption, entrepreneurial energy and emotions.

SHAPING DEVELOPMENT RESPONSES

While organized crime is a global transnational threat and illicit flows might be global, more often than not, the roots of organized crime and illicit trafficking are quintessentially local, and are invested in the communities from which they originate and transit. The value in a shift towards more perceptions-driven data is that it reflects a greater orientation towards human security, and working in partnership with local communities to address what is most important to them. Within an integrated response, therefore, there must necessarily be interventions that address organized crime itself. But, in contrast to security approaches that seek to rapidly neutralise threats, the development responses should also address the impact that organized crime has on individuals and communities, and the conditions that allow it to flourish. Development approaches are long-term goals determined on the basis of the country context to reflect local conditions.

Whereby international development is typically state centric, in responding to organized crime, space has to be made for community driven, bottom-up approaches to that are fundamentally people-centric, and that ameliorate the socio-economic impacts of organized crime on the vulnerable. In practice, these principles have resulted in an emphasis on good governance, capacity building and engagement with civil society. Development actors play a role in increasing knowledge of organized crime and its risks, and ensuring civil society has the skills to respond. However, the actual response is left to local actors, which promotes ownership and sustainability. For example, a United States Agency for International Development (USAID) strategic framework has proposed raising awareness and building civil society to put pressure on the government to address organized crime.[18] Similarly, in many regions there has been great investment made in building the capacity of independent media and journalism to investigate and report on organized crime.

At the same time, however, interventions targeted at the state still remain relevant. If the long-term goal is to undermine the currency that criminal groups have gained with local populations, then rebuilding the state as a relevant and effective entity will be critical. Emphasis here tends to focus on protecting the political process; modernising and strengthening law enforcement and the judiciary and supporting economic and social development.[19] None of these are easy or small tasks, and in each case effort has to be made to ensure that these interventions are 'crime-sensitive', which means that they are cognisant of the political-economy interests behind the flows and work to break down those linkages to criminal behaviour rather than reinforcing it.[20] The reality is likely to be highly specific to the local context, and will require a combination of international, regional and national leadership, commitment and investment over time.

CONCLUSION

This is arguably a pivotal moment in the evolutions of policies in this area. The approval of the SDGs and the parallel shifts in development financing regulations firstly firmly place organized crime within the mandate of development actors and begin to remove some of the obstacles that had previously held back development actors from engaging. The evidence basis is strengthening around a number of topics critical to understanding organized crime and its impact on development, and conversations are shifting away from long-standing stalemates around drug trafficking, violence and fragile states, towards a broader and much more nuanced agenda. A number of states have already advanced in experimenting and innovating with new responses to organized crime focused on mitigating harm, though in the majority of cases it is too early to judge their results.

Despite these positive advancements, at the same time key instruments and agreements remain lacking, including the means by which to define, design and measure successful development efforts to counter organized crime. These will be critical to ensuring that the next generation of people-centric responses to organized crime have the capacity to build resilience of communities and promote human security, the rule of law and sustainable development as part of a strategic and integrated approach.

Notes

1. 'Taking Control: Pathways to drug policies that work', *Global Commission on Drug Policy*, September 2014.
2. 'New frontiers or old boundaries? Reconsidering Approaches to the Security and Development Nexus in the Context of Responses to Organized Crime, Conflict, and Insurgency', *Global Initiative against Transnational Organized Crime* (Geneva: Global Initiative against Transnational Organized Crime, 2015).
3. This has been the conclusion of an ongoing process facilitated by the Global Initiative against Transnational Organized Crime with development donors since 2013. Reports of those meetings can be read here: http://www.globalinitiative.net/the-development-dialogue. It was also reiterated at a meeting hosted by the United Nations University in July 2015.
4. For more on the evolving development finance structure and implications for security and justice issues, see: http://www.oecd.org/dac/stats/documentupload/DCD-DAC(2014)35-ENG.pdf and http://www.oecd.org/dac/OECD%20DAC%20HLM%20Communique.pdf.
5. Mark Shaw, 'Drug trafficking in Guinea-Bissau, 1998–2014: the evolution of an elite protection network', *Journal of Modern African Studies,* vol. 53, no. 3, September 2015; Davin O'Regan and Peter Thompson, *Advancing Stability and Reconciliation in Guinea-Bissau: Lessons from Africa's first narco-state* (Washington, DC: Africa Center for Strategic Studies, 2013).

6. Marcena Hunter and Tuesday Reitano, *Composite Measures for Organised Crime: a discussion paper* (Geneva: Global Initiative against Transnational Organized Crime, unpublished).

7. 'Transforming our World: The 2030 Agenda for Sustainable Development', *United Nations (UN)* (New York: United Nations, 2015).

8. UN, Report of the Inter-Agency Expert Group on Sustainable Development Goal Indicators (E/CN.3/2016/2/Rev.1), Annex IV, https://sustainabledevelopment.un.org/content/documents/11803Official-List-of-Proposed-SDG-Indicators.pdf.

9. Dev Kar and Joseph Spanjers, *Illicit Financial Flows from Developing Countries: 2003–2012* (Washington, DC: Global Financial Integrity, 2014).

10. James Boyce and Léonce Ndikumana, *Capital Flight from Sub-Saharan African Countries: Updated Estimates, 1970–2010* (Amherst, MA: University of Massachusetts, 2012).

11. 'World Development Indicators 2014', *World Bank* (Washington, DC: World Bank Group, 2014).

12. Samantha Richmond and Carmen Alpin, 'Governments falter in the fight to curb corruption', *Afrobarometer*, 2013.

13. 'Track it, Stop it, Get it: Illicit Financial Flows from Africa', *United Nations Economic Commission for Africa (UNECA) High Level Panel on Illicit Financial Flows from Africa* (Addis Ababa: AU / UNECA Conference of Ministers, 2015).

14. 'Corridor of Violence: The Guatemala-Honduras Border', *Latin America Report N°52* (Brussels: International Crisis Group, 2014).

15. Jan Van Dijk, 'Mafia markers: assessing Organised crime and its impact upon societies', *Trends in Organised Crime*, vol. 10, no. 4, 2007, 39–56; 'Homicide Report 2013', *UNODC*.

16. Hunter and Reitano, *Composite Measures for Organised Crime*.

17. *Border Security Needs Assessment: Mali, Niger and Burkina Faso* (Copenhagen: Danish Demining Group, 2014).

18. 'The Development Response to Drug Trafficking in Africa: A Programming Guide', *USAID* (Washington, DC: USAID, 2013).

19. Camino Kavanagh, *Getting Smart and Scaling Up: Responding to the Impact of Organized Crime on Governance in Developing Countries* (New York: Centre for International Cooperation, 2013).

20. James Cockayne, 'Chasing Shadows: Strategic Responses to Organised Crime in Conflict-Affected Situations', *The RUSI Journal*, vol. 158, no. 2, April 2013.

CHAPTER 6

A State-Building Response to Organized Crime, Illicit Economies, Hybrid Threats, and Hybrid Governance

Vanda Felbab-Brown

Abstract In the chapter the author highlights the undesirable outcomes of doctrinaire law enforcement approaches and offers recommendations for the adoption of multifaceted policy responses. She argues that in order to design effective policy responses to organized crime and appropriately structure external assistance, it is important to stop thinking about crime solely as aberrant social activity to be suppressed, but instead think of crime as competition in state-making. A recognition that states often directly, not just indirectly foster and use crime, is equally important for devising successful strategies. In strong states that effectively address the needs of their societies, non-state entities cannot outcompete the state on a large scale. But in areas of socio-political marginalisation and poverty, non-state actors do—and they thus gain legitimacy within society.

Keywords Crime • State-building • Hybrid • Development

V. Felbab-Brown (✉)
The Brookings Institution, Washington, DC, USA

© The Author(s) 2018
V. Comolli (ed.), *Organized Crime and Illicit Trade*,
https://doi.org/10.1007/978-3-319-72968-8_6

121

In order to design effective policy responses to organized crime and appropriately structure external assistance for dealing with it, it is important to stop thinking about crime solely as an aberrant social activity to be suppressed, but instead think of crime as competition in state-making. A recognition that states often directly, not just indirectly foster and use crime, is equally important for developing successful policies. In strong states that effectively address the needs of their societies, non-state entities cannot outcompete the state on a large scale. But in areas of socio-political marginalisation and poverty, non-state actors do—and they thus gain legitimacy with society.

In areas of state weakness and under-provision of public goods, the effective state strategy toward organized crime is thus not merely one of law enforcement agencies to suppress crime. Approaches such as *mano dura* (iron fist), that is, zero-tolerance policies, saturation of areas with law enforcement officers, especially if they are corrupt and inadequately trained, or highly repressive measures rarely tend to be effective in suppressing organized crime and often only attack the symptoms of the social crisis, rather than its underlying conditions. This is all the more the case in areas where the state and elites choose to outsource governance to organized crime groups and gangs or relegate such areas to militant groups, rather than mobilise their own and state resources for governance.

An appropriate response is a multifaceted statebuilding effort that seeks to strengthen the bonds between the state and marginalised communities dependent on or vulnerable to participation in the drug trade and other illicit economies for reasons of economic survival and physical insecurity. The goal of anti-organized crime efforts should not only be to narrowly suppress the symptoms of illegality and state weakness, such as illicit crops or smuggling, but rather to reduce the threat that the drug trade poses from a national security concern to one of a public safety problem that does not threaten the state or the society at large.

Moreover, the design of external policy assistance must be cognisant of the fact that it is unrealistic to expect that outside policy interventions can eradicate all organized crime and illicit economies in a particular place or, for that matter, all drug trade in that place. Prioritising policies to mitigate the most dangerous forms of criminality is important, as is designing policies closely in line with the absorptive capacity of the target state. Policy interventions to reduce organized crime and to suppress any emergent crime-terror nexus can only be effective if there is a genuine commitment and participation by recipient governments and sufficient buy-in from local communities—that is, if they both find it in their interest to wean themselves off crime.

Adopting Multifaceted Approaches

Such a multifaceted approach requires that the state addresses all the complex reasons why populations turn to illegality, including law enforcement deficiencies and physical insecurity, economic poverty, and social marginalisation. Efforts need to focus on ensuring that peoples and communities will obey laws—by increasing the likelihood that illegal behaviour and corruption will be punished, but also by creating the social, economic, and political environment in which the laws are consistent with the needs of the people so that the laws can be seen as legitimate and hence be internalised. That in turn requires that elites and the state themselves undertake a fundamental reckoning of their attitudes, behavior, and policies and redesign the social contract toward greater inclusion.

In the case of the suppression of illicit economies, one key aspect of such a multifaceted approach that seeks to strengthen the bonds between the state and society and, at the same time, weaken the bonds between marginalised populations and criminal and armed actors is *the proper sequencing of suppression* and the development of economic alternatives. For many years, the United States has emphasised suppression of the illicit economies, such as forced eradication of illicit crops, above and prior to the development of legal alternatives, such as rural development or alternative livelihoods efforts. Such a counter-narcotics approach has been at odds with—in fact, the reverse of—the policy enacted by the European Union and many individual Western European countries. Such sequencing and emphasis has also been at odds with the lessons learned from the most successful rural development effort in the context of illicit crop cultivation, Thailand. Indeed, that Southeast Asian country is the only example where rural development succeeded in eliminating illicit crop cultivation.[1]

Effective economic development—be it for urban or rural spaces—does require not only proper sequencing with suppression policies and security, but also a well-funded, long-lasting, and comprehensive development approach that centres on the creation of legal jobs—always the single hardest developmental challenge whether in Nigeria's Niger Delta or Rio de Janeiro's slums. In the context of a massive youth bulge, such as in West Africa, creating legal jobs will be very hard in light of pervasive unemployment or underemployment, taxation systems that favour capital-intensive industries, and elite capture of political and economic rule-making.

Moreover, development efforts need to address all the structural drivers of why communities participate in illegal economies—such as access to markets and their development, deficiencies in infrastructure and irrigation systems, access to microcredit, and the establishment of value-added chains, and not merely search the replacement crop.

It is critical that such social interventions are designed as comprehensive rural development or comprehensive urban planning efforts, not simply limited handouts or buyoffs. The latter approaches fail—whether conducted in Medellín as a part of the demobilisation process of the former paramilitaries some of whom returned as *bandas criminales*, in Rio de Janeiro's favelas, or in Ciudad Juarez under its flagship *Todos Somos Juarez* development programme to build societal resilience against organized crime. The handout and buyoff shortcuts often also paradoxically strengthen criminal and belligerent entities and set up difficult-to-break perverse social equilibria where criminal entities continue to control marginalised segments of society while striking a let-live bargain with the state, under which criminal actors even control territories and limit state access.[2]

An effective multifaceted response by the state also entails other components:

- addressing street crime to restore communities' associational capacity. This dimension is often neglected in external assistance policies, which overwhelmingly tend to privilege broad-stroke economic assistance or the development of specialised interdiction units;
- providing access to dispute resolution and justice mechanisms, including informal or less formal ones, such as Colombia's *casas de justicia*;
- building resilience against penetration and capture by organized crime within the local political system by engaging with political parties and reinforcing less corrupt politicians;[3]
- encouraging protection of human rights, reconciliation, and nonviolent approaches;
- improving access to effective education as well as health care—a form of investment in human capital;
- insulating informal economies from takeover by the state and limiting the capacity of criminal groups to become poly-crime franchises; and
- creating public spaces free of violence and repression in which civil society can recreate its associational capacity and social capital; and otherwise fostering civil society resistance to criminal groups and *a culture of illegality*.

An effort to boost the capacity of communities to resist coercion and co-optation by criminal enterprises, however, does not mean that the state can rely on communities to tackle crime, especially violent organized crime, on their own. In fact, there is a great deal of danger in the state attempting to mobilise civil society to take on crime prematurely while the state is not yet capable of assuring the protection of the people. Without the state's ability to back up communities and protect them from retaliatory violence by organized crime or militant groups, civil society's resistance will quickly collapse. The population will not provide intelligence to the state under such circumstance. And actionable and accurate human intelligence is often critical for success of not only counterinsurgency, but also anti-organized crime efforts. Equally significant, the community can all the more sour on the state. If a state's effort to mobilise civil society to resist organized crime ends with the civil society massacred by organized crime, with its leaders assassinated, it will then be very hard for the state to mobilise civil society the second time around and restore trust in state capacity and commitment. Such mistakes in anti-organized crime policies are very costly and difficult to correct. Society will always place the burden of responsibility for violence on the state for its inability to reduce it, rather than on the criminals. During periods of intense and persistent violence, civil society may even start calling for an accommodation between the state and criminal actors.

A *concentration of resources*, both non-corrupt law enforcement and socio-economic efforts to strengthen communities, often improves the chance that the state will succeed in such a complex undertaking. Yet, it is very hard politically to concentrate resources and tackle organized crime neighbourhood by neighbourhood and illegal economies municipality by municipality. Under conditions of acute budgetary and law enforcement asset scarcity, justifying why a community is deserving of a comprehensive state assistance while others go resource-hungry (sometimes literally) is extremely difficult for government authorities. In a democracy where votes matter, the pressure to give everyone a little bit instead of concentrating resources to particular intervention areas will be all the more tempting politically.

But spreading resources over extensive areas—as much as they may be acutely in need of intervention—without achieving the necessary law enforcement and socio-economic development momentum in any place greatly augments chances of policy failure. Limited political handouts may improve the life of a community to some extent—a marginalised community is likely to be better off with 25 hospital beds instead of 20 and with an electric generator than without—but such limited state interventions will not be sufficient to alter the basic economic patterns and their political effects in a community.

Critically, the associational and organisational capacity and social action potential of communities becomes extremely quickly eviscerated during intense violence. It may well be that the *narcos* are killing each other, but when they do so on streets of cities or rural areas where the population lives, they also hollow out the communities. The bullets may only be flying overhead, but they are still deeply injuring the community underneath. Often, success hinges on the state's ability to bring violence down to start with: without a reduction in violence, socio-economic interventions do not have a chance to take off and even institutional reforms become difficult to sustain as political support weakens.

Inadequate *implementation* can kill the best strategy. Effective implementation crucially, though not exclusively depends on how operationalisation corresponds to local cultural and institutional settings.

All such social interventions require careful and consistent monitoring and the ability to correct and restructure policy that is not effective. Both the monitoring and policy adaptation are often very difficult to institutionalize effectively. They require a certain density of government oversight assets, such as embassy officials tasked with development aid or law enforcement policies, who have sufficient capacity to monitor contractors and non-governmental organisation (NGO) implementors and who have sufficient distance from policy design to not to be threatened by highlighting ineffective and counterproductive policy elements.

RETHINKING EXTERNAL ASSISTANCE

Many of the above policies suggest a considerable expansion and reconceptualisation of external assistance policies the United States (U.S.) and the European Union (EU) have taken toward combatting organized crime and drug trafficking in other parts of the world, such as West Africa and Latin America. Both have recognised the need to expand assistance to West Africa to combat organized crime. There, for example, such external assistance policies have specified several objectives: (1) to suppress the nexus of militancy-terrorism-and-organized-crime in the region and its spill-overs and leakages into Europe and reduce the chances of terrorist targeting of U.S. and European citizens in the region; (2) to suppress any potentially destabilising effects of organized crime on often already unstable and problematic governments in the region; (3) to suppress drug flows, and (4) to foster economic development in the region which criminality and organized crime can undermine.[4] The EU has launched several initiatives, the largest of which is the €22 million Cocaine Route Programme that focuses mainly on airport and sea-based interdiction in the region.[5] Since 2008, the European Union has sought to integrate anti-drug-trafficking programming into its economic assistance for the Economic Community of West African States (ECOWAS) under its *European Development Fund* to support implementation of the drug action plan adopted by ECOWAS States in Praia in December 2008. Nonetheless, many of its direct anti-organized crime and counternarcotic efforts have prioritised mainly interdiction efforts.

Between 2009 and 2012, U.S. counternarcotic assistance to West Africa amounted to US$142.5m, with an additional US$50m allocated for 2013 under the West Africa Cooperative Security Initiative.[6] The United States Agency for International Development (USAID) produced an excellent nuanced document for context-specific anti-organized-crime programming in Africa, *The Development Response to Drug Trafficking in Africa: A Programming Guide*.[7] Overall, however, the dominant U.S. response to drug trafficking in West Africa to has been to build special interdiction units (SIUs) in the region.

Indeed, SIUs are a favoured tool of U.S. and United Kingdom (UK) law enforcement assistance. In the context of highly-corrupt and inadequate law enforcement capacities, such as in West Africa, SIUs are often the only policy instrument easily available; and it is a form of assistance that the U.S. Drug Enforcement Administration has experience in delivering abroad. Sometimes, SIUs can score a spectacular success[8] and can have deep impact on rooting out corruption and weakening organized crime. One of the most effective special law enforcement and prosecution units was The Directorate of Special Operations (or Scorpions) in South Africa between 2001 and 2009. Rather than merely a special interdiction unit, the Scorpions were a multidisciplinary agency within the National Prosecuting Authority in South Africa, comprising 536 of the country's best prosecutors, police, and financial, forensic and intelligence experts who investigated and prosecuted organized crime and corruption. An international version of such a special investigative unit (and tribunal) is The International Commission Against Impunity in Guatemala (*La Comisión Internacional Contra La Impunidad en Guatemala* or CICIG) that has managed to effectively prosecute entrenched corruption and organized crime in a political system deeply pervaded by crime and thick connections between politicians, law enforcement forces, and criminals.[9]

Yet despite these and other important successes, narrowly-focused special interdiction units focused on seizure and disruption are often of limited overall effectiveness. Moreover, and dangerously, they can end up going rogue.[10] Within intensely corrupt political systems with powerful criminal organisations, the political and coercion pressures on SIUs, just like on ordinary law enforcement units and police departments, can be irresistible, particularly if foreign assistance and monitoring ceases. After all, the best way to become a country's top drug traffickers is to be the top counter-narcotics unit, just as the best way to be the top capo is to be the minister of counternarcotics, intelligence, or justice—as China's minister of counternarcotics Du Yuesheng in the 1930s, Peru's intelligence czar Vladimiro Montesinos in the 1990s, and Mexico's drug czar José de Jesús Gutiérrez Rebollo and the elite counter-narcotics unit, the Zetas, that same decade all learned. With superior training, they can prevail against their criminal rivals and capture the criminal markets, while hiding their rogue activities under the cloak of law enforcement. Conversely, if such elite SIUs are effective in taking on organized crime and its political backers and do promote rule of law, the political will within the host country to maintain and support the SIU can dissipate quickly. Thus after the Scorpions in South Africa came to investigate corrupt deals of top-level politicians, such as then Deputy President Jacob Zuma, they were rapidly disbanded, absorbed into other law enforcement departments, gutted of power, and eventually withered.[11] When external actors do engage in building SIUs abroad, they need from the beginning to build into their operational plans strategies to dismantle and roll back SIUs they created if they go rogue or if the host country political will to support them evaporates. At a minimum, such units require constant diligent monitoring and possibly disciplinary action by their foreign sponsors for many years.

Overall, external assistance partners need to approach anti-crime assistance with considerable caution. Rather than rushing to assist wherever organized crime reaches visibility, the U.S., the EU, and other potential partners need to adopt a do-no-harm rule, with a systematic evaluation of the side-effects of their policy actions prominently built into consideration of policy options. Apart from smart design based on a state-building conceptualisation of fighting organized crime and careful implementation, policy design thus must be keenly cognisant of the fact that it is unrealistic to expect that external interventions can eradicate all organized crime and illicit economies in a particular place or, for that matter, all drug trafficking in that place.

The priority for the United States and the international community needs to be to combat the most disruptive and dangerous networks of organized crime and belligerency. Such networks are those with the greatest links or potential links to international terrorist groups with global reach. Indeed, there is a considerable variation in the capacity of organized crime groups to penetrate new territories, as Federico Varese has shown,[12] or new domains. Hardly all criminal groups are poly-crime enterprises: smuggling cocaine is not the same as smuggling fissile material. Although it is frequently suggested that organized crime groups will easily make alliances or without restraint cooperate with terrorist and militant groups, the relationship between the two kinds of actors is often fraught and violent.[13] Most organized crime groups are not simply blind profit maximisers, they also weigh risks, including the risk of falling into cahoots with militant groups and thus drawing a far different level of scrutiny and repression from law enforcement.

Similarly, terrorist groups are not uniform in their capacities to penetrate new territories and sustain their operating bases there without triggering a backlash from local populations. In Mali and Syria, Salafi groups succeeded in rapidly appropriating local causes for their global jihad purpose. In Iraq al-Qaeda initially succeeded in anchoring itself among the Sunni population until U.S. efforts fostered a Sunni rebellion against it. In Pakistan, al-Qaeda and other Salafi groups' ability to take over or appropriate local actors has varied considerably and also stirred tribal rebellions and tribal anti-al-Qaeda militias. In Somalia, al-Qaeda struggled to establish itself there in the 1990s, eventually gave up, and ultimately its presence came rather through a reverse process: a native Somali jihadi group, al-Shabaab, embracing the global Salafi cause and embracing al-Qaeda[14] and later flirting with embracing on the Islamic State.[15] Rather than assuming uniformity in motivations and capabilities of terrorists and criminals, their convergence toward a strategic alliance or nexus, or treating the two as a monolith,[16] external assistance policy efforts need to be guided by strict prioritisation, understanding the nuances between those actors, and seeking to divide them and push them apart.

The criminal networks that the United States and the international community should prioritise in targeting, however, also include those that are most rapacious and predatory to the society and state and most concentrate rents from illicit economies to a narrow clique of people, whether linked to the state or anti-state militant group. Not only are those most reprehensible, they also most undermine internal stability and create the conditions for militant groups to establish themselves among local populations.

The above two criteria—criminal groups linked to terrorist organisations and the most predatory criminal groups perpetuating marginalisation and exclusion and further reducing the legitimacy of the state—may at times be in conflict and thus pose a difficult policy dilemma.[17] In addition to considering the severity of the threat posed to the international community and to the host state and society, the estimated effectiveness of policy intervention with respect to each type of group needs to be factored into the analysis of such policy choices.

UNDESIRABLE OUTCOMES OF INDISCRIMINATE LAW ENFORCEMENT

It is important to realise that indiscriminate and uniform application of law enforcement—whether external or internal—can generate several undesirable outcomes that need to be guarded against. First, the weakest criminal groups can be eliminated through such an approach, with law enforcement inadvertently increasing the efficiency, lethality, and coercive and corruption power of the remaining criminal groups operating in the region.

Second, such an application of law enforcement without prioritisation can indeed push criminal groups into an alliance with terrorist groups—the opposite of what should be the purpose of law enforcement and especially outside policy intervention. Both outcomes have repeatedly emerged in various regions of the world as a result of opportunistic, non-strategic drug interdiction and law enforcement policies.

Third, there is a substantial risk that some recipient governments will come to see international counter-narcotics or anti-organized crime aid as yet another form of rent to be acquired for their power and profit maximisation, in the same way that anti-Communist or counterterrorism aid had often been seen. Such funds can be diverted for personal profits; or worse yet against domestic political opposition and undermine institutional development and effective and accountable governance in the country.

Fourth, building up law enforcement capacity and intervening against illicit economies may often been perceived by local populations as antagonistic to their interests. Such a misalignment between state and societal interests may at a minimum limit the effectiveness of policy intervention; and at worst compromise other, more important U.S. and international interests, such as to reduce violent conflict and suppress terrorism.

The international community can limit these dangers by following some overarching guiding principles regarding extending outside assistance to suppress organized crime.

International assistance should be carefully calibrated to the absorptive capacity of the partner country. In places where state capacity is minimal and law enforcement often deeply corrupt, an initial focus on strengthening police capacity to fight street crime, reducing corruption, and increasing the effectiveness and reach of the justice system may be the optimal initial interventions.

Blanket policies to fight corruption abroad and pre-canned rule-of-law programmes are often likely to be ineffective, particularly within political systems deeply pervaded by corruption and built around patronage networks.[18] Moreover, anti-corruption efforts, like anti-crime and counter-narcotics efforts, can easily be exploited by recipient governments to undermine or eliminate their political opponents. Beyond altruistically promoting good governance, international anti-corruption assistance should seek out political actors who will benefit from bucking existing corruption-prone political processes and genuinely embracing authentic anti-corruption efforts. The next crucial step, however, is to make sure that beyond individual political expedience and being adopted as political tools, such practices become an ingrained habit of the political system—in other words, are institutionalised beyond particular politicians and particular government administrations. Identifying other stakeholders who also will benefit from virtuous behaviour, such as businesses or NGOs that profit economically or can gain in status and reputation by not being corrupt, is crucial.

Only once careful monitoring by outside actors has determined that anti-crime or anti-corruption assistance has been positively incorporated, can it be fruitful to increase assistance for anti-organized crime efforts, including advanced-technology transfers and training. Careful monitoring of all anti-organized crime programmes—including their effects on the internal political arrangements and power distribution within the society and their intended effects on the power of criminal groups and their links to terrorist groups—needs to be consistently conducted by outside actors.

International anti-crime assistance strategy needs to be built around a broad state-building and focus and emphasise fostering good governance. Ultimately, policy interventions to reduce organized crime and to suppress any emergent crime-terror nexus can only be effective if there is a genuine commitment and participation by recipient governments and sufficient buy-in from local communities.

NOTES

1. For details, see, for example, Ronald D. Renard, *Opium Reduction in Thailand, 1970–2000: A Thirty-Year Journey* (Bangkok: UN Drug Control Programme Silkworm Books, 2001) and Pierre-Arnaud Chouvy, *Opium: Uncovering the Politics of Poppy* (London: I.B. Taurus, 2009), pp. 63–93.

2. See, for example, Enrique Desmond Arias, 'Trouble en Route: Drug Trafficking and Clientelism in Rio de Janeiro Shantytowns', *Qualitative Sociology*, vol. 29, no. 4, 2006, pp. 427–445.

3. For an excellent discussion of how to launch and expand such difficult and complicated efforts and identify partners for engagement in the context of pervasive corruption, see Camino Kavanagh, *Getting Smart and Scaling Up: Responding to the Impact of Organised Crime on Governance in Developing Countries* (New York: Centre for International Cooperation, 2013); and Brooke Stearns Lawson and Phyllis Dininio, 'The Development Response to Drug Trafficking in Africa: A Programming Guide', *USAID*, April 2013, http://www.usaid.gov/sites/default/files/documents/1860/Development_Response_to_Drug_Trafficking_in_Africa_Programming_Guide.pdf.

4. Author's interviews with US officials of the Department of State, Washington, DC, August 2012, of the Drug Enforcement Administration, Nairobi, April 2013, and UK officials of the Department for International Development, London, May 2013. See also, Cecilia Malmström, 'The External Dimension of EU-Police Cooperation in West African Countries –Towards Global and Integrated International Policing', *Press Release Database*, SPEECH/10/505, 30 September 2010, http://europa.eu/rapid/press-release_SPEECH-10-505_en.htm and 'Long-term Responses to Global Security Threats: Contributing to Security Capacity Building in Third Countries through the Instrument for Stability', *European Commission*, March 2011, https://ec.europa.eu/europeaid/sites/devco/files/publication-long-term-responses-global-security-threats-2011_en.pdf.

5. For more details see 'Cocaine Route Programme', *European Union*, http://www.cocaineroute.eu/.

6. Charlie Savage and Thom Shanker, 'U.S. Drug War Expands to Africa, a Newer Hub for Cartels', *New York Times*, 21 July 2012; and 'Memorandum for the Secretary of State: Presidential Determination on Major Drug Transit or Major Illicit Drug Producing Countries for Fiscal Year 2014', *The White House, Office of the Press Secretary, Presidential Determination No. 2013–14*, 13 September 2013, http://iipdigital.usembassy.gov/st/english/texttrans/2013/09/20130913282879.html#ixzz2glhlmqC1.

7. Stearns Lawson and Dininio, 'The Development Response to Drug Trafficking in Africa: A Programming Guide'.

8. Adam Nossiter, 'U.S. Sting That Snared Guinea-Bissau Ex-Admiral Shines Light on Drug Trade', *New York Times*, 15 April 2013, http://www.nytimes.com/2013/04/16/world/africa/us-sting-that-snared-guinea-bissau-ex-admiral-shines-light-on-drug-trade.html?_r=0.

9. For an evaluation of CICIG's effectiveness, see, for example, 'La Comisión Internacional Contra La Impunidad en Guatemala: Un Estudio de Investigación de WOLA Sobre La Experiencia de la CICIG', *Washington Office on Latin America (WOLA)*, March 2015, http://www.wola.org/sites/default/files/CICIG%203.25.pdf.

10. Vanda Felbab-Brown, *Despite Its Siren Song, High-Value Targeting Doesn't Fit All: Matching Interdiction Patterns to Specific Narcoterrorism and Organized-Crime Contexts* (Washington DC: The Brookings Institution, 1 October 2013).

11. For a detailed evaluation of the Scorpions' history and effectiveness, see, for example, Joey Berning and Moses Montesh, 'Countering Corruption in South Africa: The Rise and Fall of the Scorpions and the Hawks', *South Africa Crime Quarterly*, March 2012, pp. 3–10.

12. Federico Varese, *Mafias on the Move* (Princeton, NJ: Princeton University Press, 2011).

13. See, for example, Douglas Farah, 'Fixers, Superfixers, and Shadow Facilitators: How Networks Connect', in Jacqueline Brewer and Michael Miklaucic (eds.), *Convergence: Illicit Networks and National Security in the Age of Globalization* (Washington DC: NDU Press, 2013); Felbab-Brown, *Shooting Up: Counterinsurgency and the War on Drugs*.

14. Kenneth Menkhaus and Jacob Shapiro, 'Non-state Actors and Failed States: Lessons from Al Qaeda's Experiences in the Horn of Africa', in Anne Clunan and Harold Trinkunas (eds.), *Ungoverned Spaces: Alternatives to State Authority in an Era of Softened Sovereignty* (Stanford, CA: Stanford University Press, 2010).

15. As of summer of 2015, different factions within al-Shabaab had divergent opinions on whether to identify with the Islamic State. Author's fieldwork in Somalia, spring 2015. See also, Vanda Felbab-Brown, 'Saving Somalia (Again)', *Foreign Affairs*, June 2015, https://www.foreignaffairs.com/articles/somalia/2015-06-23/saving-somalia-again; and Stig Jarle Hansen, *Al Shabaab in Somalia: The History and Ideology of a Militant Islamist Group* (Oxford: Oxford University Press, 2013).

16. For such analyses, see, for example, Tamara Makarenko, 'The Crime–Terror Continuum: Tracing the Interplay between Transnational Organised Crime and Terrorism', *Global Crime*, vol. 6, no. 1, February 2004, pp.129–145; Peng Wang, 'The Crime-Terror Nexus: Transformation,

Alliance, Convergence', *Asian Social Sciences*, vol. 6, 2010, pp. 11–20; Chris Dishman, 'The Leaderless Nexus: When Crime and Terror Converge', *Studies in Conflict and Terrorism*, vol. 28, no. 3, 2005, pp. 237–252. See also Micklaucic and Brewer (eds.), *Convergence: Illicit Networks and National Security in the Age of Globalization*.

17. How this conflict produced ineffective and counterproductive U.S. counterterrorism and state-building policies in Afghanistan, see Vanda Felbab-Brown, *Aspiration and Ambivalence: Strategies and Realities of Counterinsurgency and State-Building in Afghanistan* (Washington DC: The Brookings Institution Press, 2012).

18. See, for example, Rachel Kleinfeld, *Advancing the Rule of Law Abroad: Next Generation Reform* (Washington DC: Carnegie Endowment for International Peace, 2012).

CONCLUSION

Abstract In the concluding chapter the editor brings together common treads that had emerged throughout the book. A message that transpires strongly is that organized crime is nothing less than a strategic challenge.

The chapter also reflects on local responses. The local-level dimension is one that in the era of globalisation is often forgotten or, at a minimum, is not given enough attention. Recognising the strategic nature of the organized crime challenge should not preclude local initiatives and favour only country or region-wide strategies.

Keywords Crime • Resilience • Capacity building

If there is one strong—common—message that should emerge from the preceding discussion is that organized crime is nothing less than a strategic challenge. No matter from which angle one looks at the problem. It could be illicit trade and its impact on licit business, or the relationship between the state and criminals or between criminal actors and society, or it could be from the point of view of cyber and technological exploitation

V. Comolli
International Institute for Strategic Studies
London, UK

or, finally, it could be through assessing socio-economic development in conflict or fragile states. The evidence is abundant, although measuring the *true* impact of organized crime remains challenging. Counting arrests and seizures might still be the preferred approach in some circles but, in truth, those statistics tell us very little and certainly do no provide a strategic picture.

It is also no surprise that all contributors to this volume make reference to governance, the environment, public health and security—building a common tread—among the areas that are threatened by various forms of criminal activities and their knock-on effects. All societies of the world have come to face these challenges and some, more than others—and in spite of the transnational nature of organized crime—appear to be bearing the largest brunt. In fact, most Western individuals would hardly ever come into contact with organized crime in the course of their lives, and although London, Paris or New York are far from immune from this phenomenon very few would get in contact with it directly (or knowingly). Moreover, unlike the media attention received by terrorist attacks, the actions of organized criminal networks rarely make headlines which, in turn, contributes to little public understanding of the nature and extent of the problem. As a result, it becomes harder to summon the required political willingness to take action in the face of many other pressing crises and priorities.

If this was not enough, the absence of a commonly agreed definition of organized crime hampers cooperation. Given the multiple impact of the phenomenon a broad set of actors need to engage in devising and implementing anti-organized crime initiatives: but who should be involved and indeed lead such efforts? This book makes the case against an exclusively law-enforcement or criminal justice driven strategy. Equally, it argues against any single-sector approach, being one centered on development initiatives or technological innovation. Any one of those, on its own, would be inadequate. Instead, it is only through a smartly sequenced integrated approach that the causes and implications of organized crime can be addressed. Notably, it is not only the actors devising and implementing strategies that are required to be diverse. The receiving end should be equally varied. In other words, the international community should not limit itself to interacting with (carefully selected-) state actors when engaging developing countries on anti organized crime initiatives. Civil societies, the private sector, the media and common citizens all have a role to play. Indeed, paying greater attention to people's perception of organized crime—which in some cases might enjoy a substantial level of legitimacy among disenfranchised citizens—would help tackle its root causes and encourage those who had turned to criminality to reconsider their options. None of this is a straightforward or immediate endeavor. In some Latin American or African countries, for example, this process would entail rebuilding a badly damaged social contract between the state and society, particularly where state actors themselves engage in criminal activities, are heavily corrupted and are incapable of providing services, including security, to those they are supposed to administer. Not only this creates a disconnect between people and institutions. The resulting vacuum is usually quickly filled by criminal networks, gangs, militias or violent extremists who find among local un-employed, but usually IT-savvy, youth ideal foot soldiers. More and more urban centres around the world—and primarily African, Asian and Latin American slums—are experiencing this trend raising serious concerns for the growth of licit economies as well as formal governance structures and human security.

The local-level dimension is one that in the era of globalisation is often forgotten or, at a minimum, is not given enough attention. Recognising the strategic nature of the organized crime challenge should not preclude local initiatives and favour only country or region-wide strategies. To mention one case, much has been said about illicit trafficking across the Sahel and its links to violent extremism and conflict. Given long-established smuggling routes across the region, the involvement of nomadic tribes and porous borders, regional approaches appear to be the ones more likely to bear results. I too agree that initiatives that focus on one country alone might be ineffective and indeed could result in the so-called balloon effect displacing the problem to neighboring countries. A series of interviews conducted with law-enforcement practitioners and researchers during a trip to Mali however highlighted the extent to which criminal activities were closely linked to specific localities and families or clans, and how local dynamics prevailed over regional ones. This suggested that a region-wide approach was unlikely to be able to capture and address dynamics pertinent to specific towns or local groups. The other problem that this highlighted concerned data collection. This book makes abundantly clear the difficulties of measuring organized crime in general. Language and cultural barriers add an additional layer of complication and emphasise, once more, the importance of engaging local non-state actors such as civil societies that are trusted among local communities and, as a result, are better placed than any well-meaning Western partner to collect information and form an understating of criminal dynamics in a given region.[1]

Some progress has been made and some lessons have been learnt which have prompted more nuanced and comprehensive discussions around the problem of organized crime, including through placing the issue on the development agenda. This has been an important step forward but given the complexity of the threat and the multiplicity of areas affected by organized crime much more is needed. Comprehensively measuring organized crime and its impacts will remain a challenge going forward but one could argue that the existing evidence is more than enough to prompt action. What is at times still missing is political will. If nothing else, including altruistic sentiments, succeeds in convincing Western political class to get involved, perhaps, as argued by Karl Lallerstedt, 'enlightened self-interest' could be the key to unlock serious action. After all, in an interdepended world, having to deal with corrupt or criminal partners is bad for business. From this point of view, supporting capacity building and helping developing nations tackle organized crime and build resilience to it are forms of insurance that could lead to a win-win situation.

NOTE

1. Interviews conducted by the author, Bamako, Mali, October 2014.

Index[1]

[1] Note: Page numbers followed by 'n' refer to notes.

© The Author(s) 2018   139
V. Comolli (ed.), *Organized Crime and Illicit Trade*,
https://doi.org/10.1007/978-3-319-72968-8

Lightning Source UK Ltd.
Milton Keynes UK
UKHW021816231219
355920UK00006B/48/P